D0851970

Siskiyou County
School Library

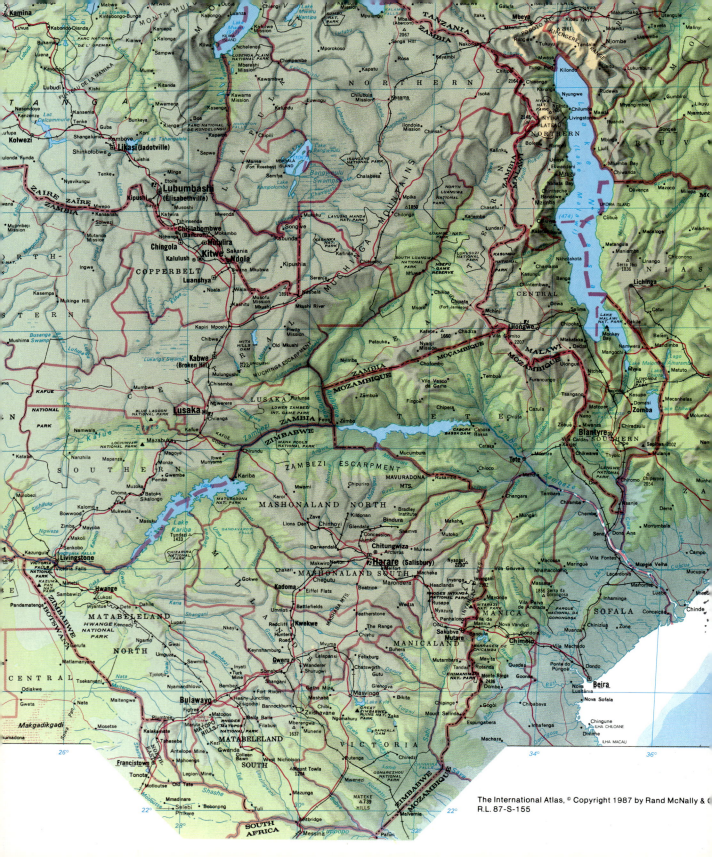

The International Atlas, © Copyright 1987 by Rand McNally & C
R.L. 87-S-155

Enchantment of the World

ZIMBABWE

By Jason Lauré

Consultant for Zimbabwe: John Rowe, Ph.D., African Studies Faculty, Northwestern University, Evanston, Illinois

Consultant for Reading: Robert L. Hillerich, Ph.D., Bowling Green State University, Bowling Green, Ohio

CHILDRENS PRESS ®

CHICAGO

A Venda chief's house

Library of Congress Cataloging-in-Publication Data

Lauré, Jason.
  Zimbabwe.

  (Enchantment of the world)
  Includes index.
  Summary: An introduction to the geography, history,
government, economy, culture, and people of the
landlocked southeastern African country, known as
Rhodesia before it gained independence in 1980.
  1. Zimbabwe—Juvenile literature. [1. Zimbabwe]
I. Title. II. Series.
DT962.L38 1988   968.91   87-35426
ISBN 0-516-02704-2

Childrens Press®, Chicago
Copyright ©1988 by Regensteiner Publishing Enterprises, Inc.
All rights reserved. Published simultaneously in Canada.
Printed in the United States of America.
1 2 3 4 5 6 7 8 9 10 R 97 96 95 94 93 92 91 90 89 88

Picture Acknowledgments
Valan Photos: © Christine Osborne: 4, 6 (top), 11 (right),
14 (right), 42 (bottom right), 78 (bottom right), 80, 84
(bottom right)
Shostal: 5, 6 (bottom), 8, 11 (left), 18 (bottom), 21 (left), 42
(top), 60, 83 (2 photos), 84 (bottom left), 87 (left), 88, 90
(top), 92, 100, 105 (left), 113
Nawrocki Stock Photo: © Jason Lauré: 9, 12 (right), 14
(left), 15, 17 (right), 41, 45 (2 photos), 52 (2 photos), 53
(left), 62 (left), 65 (2 photos), 66, 70, 71 (2 photos), 72 (2
photos), 81 (top left & bottom), 87 (right), 102, 105 (right),
112 (bottom right)
Photri: 10, 18 (top), 21 (right), 42 (bottom left), 78 (top left
& right), 79 (2 photos), 81 (top right), 82, 89 (right)
Root Resources: © Kenneth W. Fink: 12 (left); © Ted
Farrington: 86 (right); © Charles G. Summers, Jr./Colorado
Nature Photographic Studio: 86 (left), 89 (left)
© **Cameramann International, Ltd.:** Cover (both pictures),
17 (left, top & bottom), 62 (right), 68 (right), 75, 76 (top
and bottom right), 78 (bottom left), 84 (top), 90 (bottom
left), 93 (right), 96, 106 (2 photos), 112 (bottom left)
Historical Pictures Service, Chicago: 24, 25 (2 photos), 28,
30 (2 photos), 31, 34
AP/Wide World Photos: 38, 47 (2 photos), 49 (2 photos),
53 (right), 59, 94, 95, 111
JB Pictures: © Louise Gubb: 58, 68 (left), 73, 112 (top left)
Odyssey Productions © Robert Frerck: 76 (bottom left), 90
(bottom right), 93 (left), 112 (top right)
Len W. Meents: Maps on pages 58, 82, 88
**Courtesy Flag Research Center, Winchester,
Massachusetts 01890:** Flag on back cover
Cover: Center of downtown Harare; inset, rural village of
traditional homes

*Members of
the Ndebele*

TABLE OF CONTENTS

Zimbabwe has enough arable land (above) to be self-sufficient
in agriculture. Some areas with granite outcroppings (below)
are not suitable for cultivation.

Chapter 1

LANDLOCKED

LANDSCAPE

The Republic of Zimbabwe, a nation slightly smaller than California, comprises 150,804 square miles (390,580 square kilometers). Until it became independent in 1980, Zimbabwe was known as Rhodesia; its official name was Southern Rhodesia. It is located in southeastern Africa, landlocked between other countries, far from the Atlantic Ocean to the west, and from the Indian Ocean to the east.

THE LAND

Most of the interior is a high plain, or savanna, called the *highveld,* lying 3,000 to 5,000 feet (910 to 1,500 meters) above sea level. With a delightful climate, sufficient rain, and good soil, this area is well suited for farming a wide variety of crops. Although quite flat, the highveld is marked by granite outcroppings, called *kopjes.* The Great Dyke, a huge formation of mineralized rocks, runs in a narrow strip, roughly north to south, for 300 miles (483 kilometers).

From the highveld, the land slopes very gently downward through a *midveld* to sandy plains called the *lowveld,* occurring mostly in the south.

7

The Inyanga Mountains are in the distance.

A quite large portion of the southwestern section of the country receives little rainfall and is unsuitable for farming, livestock, or permanent human habitation.

The Zambezi River forms much of the north and northeast boundaries, separating the country from Zambia. Mozambique borders Zimbabwe on the north and east. South Africa is on the south, separated from Zimbabwe by the Limpopo River. Botswana is on the southwest and west, and here the Shashe River forms part of the border.

The Vumba and Inyanga mountain ranges form a barrier of more than 200 miles (322 kilometers) at Zimbabwe's eastern border. This area is marked by streams and waterfalls and Zimbabwe's highest elevation, Mount Inyangani, at 8,514 feet (2,595 meters). In the southwest are the Matopos, granite hills separated by cool valleys.

The Zambezi River is vital to Zimbabwe.

RIVERS AND LAKES

David Livingstone made the Zambezi River part of his life's work, as he was captivated with the river. Today, virtually the entire life of Zimbabwe would be very different were it not for the river. The Zambezi gives Zimbabwe much of its drama, its electricity, its water sports, and part of its actual shape.

The source of the Zambezi lies to the west of Zimbabwe, at a point where Zambia, Angola, and Zaire come together. From the drainage collected by tributaries, runoff waters gather, growing in strength and volume as the river runs eastward. As the river approaches the northwest corner of Zimbabwe, it widens gradually, until it stretches a mile across. The placid river gives no hint of what lies ahead. Immediately after reaching Zimbabwe, there is a mighty roaring rush of water as the river drops 300 feet (91 meters) at Victoria Falls. Its extraordinary width makes the

9

Lake Kariba

falls the outstanding natural physical feature of the country. The Zambezi River widens out into Lake Kariba, a 200-mile (322-kilometer) man-made lake created by the Kariba Dam.

Although practically bounded by rivers and set off by the Victoria Falls, Zimbabwe has no natural lakes. While Lake Kariba is unusually large for a man-made lake, the largest south of the Sahara Desert, many man-made lakes have been created in Zimbabwe by damming the country's many small rivers.

MINERALS

Zimbabwe's vast mineral wealth is distributed widely across the country. The Zimbabweans have been mining gold for hundreds of years, perhaps since as early as the seventh century. Today, Zimbabwe produces 500,000 ounces (12,680,000 grams) of gold a year. More than forty other minerals are found in Zimbabwe in sufficient quantities to support commercial mining activities.

Above: Women harvesting cotton
Left: An orange plantation

AGRICULTURE

A small portion of the country is considered suitable for farming, and much of that is on the highveld. The variety of crops is broad, thanks to the tropical climate and the high elevation. In the lowlands, irrigation permits other products to be grown, ranging from those found in tropical to temperate climates. These crops include the staple food, maize (corn), as well as cotton; tobacco; deciduous fruits such as apples, peaches, and pears; citrus fruits, particularly oranges; and coffee and tea.

FLORA

Important natural forests are found in the northwest portion of the country. Small stands of forest are located in the eastern highlands. Eucalyptus was introduced in the 1920s, and extensive plantations of pines are also in operation.

A baobab tree (left) and a hibiscus blossom (right)

While an enormous variety of trees, flowers, grasses, and bushes grow in Zimbabwe, a few species are especially evocative of the country. The baobab tree, which occurs elsewhere in Africa, looks very much as if it were growing upside down. The enormous trunk rises straight up and then branches off into grotesquely twisted arms ending in twigs that look more like roots. The flame lily, common throughout tropical Africa, is regarded as the country's national flower. Its delicate petals are flame orange-red in color, softening to yellow at the very base.

Jacaranda trees have been introduced to Zimbabwe and line the streets of Harare, the capital. When their purple flowers blossom without green leaves to soften their glow, the streets seem to be painted with purple. When the flowers fall, the streets become purple carpets.

Chapter 2

THE PEOPLE OF
ZIMBABWE

THE SHONA

Most African countries comprise many language or ethnic
groups forced into nationhood by lines drawn on a map. Each
brings to the nation its own personality, skills, language, and
traditions. In extreme cases there is warfare or conflict between
political or ethnic groups.

In Zimbabwe, the Shona form the majority of the people, about
80 percent of the total population. Ancestors of today's Shona
people were already living in Zimbabwe more than eight hundred
years ago. President Robert Mugabe and the people who make up
his political party are mostly Shona. Within this language group,
the people are divided into a number of different chiefdoms,
similar to the clans of Scotland. The way they speak Shona varies
too, similar to the differences in English among the British,
Americans, and Australians.

The Shona are a peaceful farming people; however, they
vigorously resisted the intrusion of whites into their territory.

A Shona chief (left) and Shona women participating in a Roman Catholic mass (right)

Their ancestral spirits, they believed, were very disturbed when the whites took over their land. Even more important, Africans were subjected to forced labor, new taxes, and racism. When a series of natural disasters occurred—drought, locusts, disease, and the death of hundreds of cattle—it seemed that the spirits were venting their anger at the whites. At this point, Africans rose in rebellion against the whites.

THE NDEBELE

Relative newcomers are the Ndebele-speakers, or Matabele, who make up about 14 percent of Zimbabwe's population. The Ndebele (pronounced in-da-BAY-lee) came into the country from the south in the early 1800s, fleeing the military forces of Shaka, the Zulu king, who then held power over the entire Zulu territory. Joshua Nkomo, who was the principal rival to Robert Mugabe, is an Ndebele. The former president of Zimbawe, which was a ceremonial position, is an Ndebele, Canaan Banana.

Former president Canaan Banana (far left)

The Ndebele are principally a cattle raising people, who also grew millet (now replaced by maize). They were also hunters, frequently attacking large, wild animals with clubs. They employed their well-organized military formations against other people. When they first entered present-day Zimbabwe, they easily dominated the more numerous Shona groups. The Shona were servants to the Ndebele and were often forced to pay tribute (a form of taxation) to them. The Ndebele often raided neighboring people, taking their cattle as plunder.

OTHER ZIMBABWEANS

There are also tiny remnants of other language groups living within Zimbabwe's national borders. Among them are the Tonga, Birwa, Venda, and Hlegwe. Together, they make up no more than 5 percent of Zimbabwe's population. All of these small groups are found in larger numbers outside Zimbabwe's borders, and many retain relationships with their kin living in other countries.

A scattering of San, known to westerners as Bushmen, sometimes live in Zimbabwe. Moving back and forth across the border that separates Zimbabwe from Botswana, the San in Zimbabwe number no more than a few hundred people. They are in every sense an endangered people because their existence is so dependent on living in perfect isolation. The San are renowned for their ability to track animals and for living on the scarce resources of the Kalahari Desert, which occupies a good portion of Botswana.

CHIEFS

Hereditary chiefs have traditionally ruled the clans within local areas, presiding over traditional courts, acting as heads of state. When the whites took over, they left the chiefdom system largely in place, but became the real decision makers. The chiefs were used to transmit messages from the white government, whose members were not seen by the people living in the rural areas. A few blacks were often not aware that whites actually ruled their country, a fact that emerged during the 1980 elections, when some asked why they needed independence.

THE WHITES

The whites, or Europeans, as they are usually referred to in Africa, make up about 1.5 percent of the total population, approximately 120,000 people. Although small in number, they were the most powerful group in Zimbabwe before independence and continue to dominate the economy today. About three-quarters of the whites are of British origin, the first of whom arrived in the 1890s. There are also numbers of Afrikaners from South Africa. After the independence of Mozambique in 1975, the

*Above: A white Zimbabwean veteran of
World War I   Left: Schoolchildren in the
David Livingstone Public School in Harare*

Europeans were joined by thousands of Portuguese who had been
living in that former Portuguese colony. Small numbers of other
Europeans, such as Italians and Greeks, also live in Zimbabwe.

ASIANS AND COLOREDS

   Living exclusively in the cities is a small number of Asians,
perhaps ten thousand in all. They came to Zimbabwe either
directly from India or from the Indian community of South Africa.
As is common in Africa, they are heavily involved in trade and
white-collar professional jobs. Finally, as is invariably the case
when blacks and whites live in close proximity, there are the
Coloreds, a term used in Africa to denote people of mixed race.
They number about thirty thousand.

Ruins of Great Zimbabwe built by the Shona from the eleventh century to the fifteenth century.

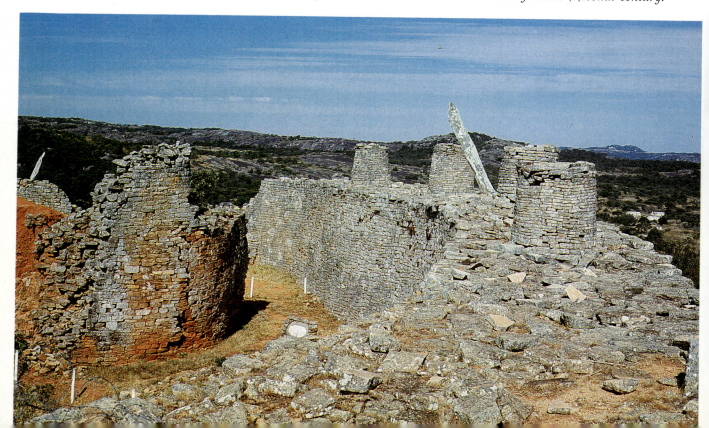

Chapter 3

ZIMBABWE'S PAST

EARLY HISTORY

An early species of man lived in central and eastern Africa some 100,000 years ago. Later, Stone Age cultures occupied the territory. About 20,000 years before Christ, early ancestors of the Khoisan people roamed the area, as hunter-gatherers.

About the fifth century A.D., Bantu-speaking pastoralists began to arrive in the area, coming from the north, coexisting with the Khoisan. This migration grew in numbers through the next centuries, culminating in a large-scale movement of people in the tenth and eleventh centuries. They had knowledge of iron working and they planted crops, and so could support a larger population than the hunters and gatherers, who gradually moved out. The area in which they settled stretched from the Zambezi to the Limpopo rivers, which today form two of the natural borders of Zimbabwe. These people were Shona speakers, ancestors of today's Shona majority. The land they occupied became known as Mashonaland.

When the Ndebele people invaded the territory in the nineteenth century, they established their own area in what was

19

western Shona territory; this became known as Matabeleland. The Ndebele, although small in numbers, overwhelmed the Shona because their disciplined warriors were organized into regiments, which gave them military superiority.

GREAT ZIMBABWE

The early Shona built Great Zimbabwe and created a huge city-state there, working and profiting from the vast reserves of gold that were found throughout the area. Architecture was one of their chief artistic expressions.

The ancestors of today's dominant Shona people were established at Great Zimbabwe by the eleventh century. Zimbabwe is a Shona word meaning "stone enclosure." Great Zimbabwe was a forerunner of a modern city, with structures for housing, markets, food storage, and religious shrines. The structures were created from stones, put together without any mortar, and have remained standing for hundreds of years. Today, you can see the long sections of double protective walls, just wide enough for a person to walk through. In the Great Enclosure is a conical tower twenty-nine feet (nine meters) high that is a mystery. No one knows what its purpose was. Low, round sections of walls indicate the corrals where cattle were kept. Although some of the site was vandalized by white treasure hunters in the 1890s, much of it remains, permitting a look directly into the past.

Great Zimbabwe was noted for the green soapstone birds that were carved and placed on top of many of the structures. These birds have been taken from the ruins and can be seen in a museum near Masvingo.

*Above: Rock paintings found
in the Chimanimani Mountains
in the southeast
Left: The mysterious conical
tower in Great Zimbabwe*

These silent structures reveal only part of their story to visitors
who are drawn to this site. In the mid-fifteenth century, the area
was abandoned because the great population had used up the
natural resources. The soil was exhausted, the timber needed for
fuel was used up, and the mines had been worked out. Of
somewhat less importance, there was a severe shortage of salt,
needed to preserve meat. Although some prefer to attribute the
desertion of Great Zimbabwe to mysterious causes, the city simply
didn't fulfill the people's needs any longer, and they moved on.

The absence of written records is often equated by the West with the absence of history itself. Yet the presence of the Great Zimbabwe ruins, which date back to the eleventh century, on a site occupied since the fifth century, proves that Africans had thriving cultures that were simply unknown—in Europe. Life in Africa did not begin with the arrival of the white man. But as was true of so many aspects of white life in black Africa, all that mattered to the whites was what they knew about their own experience. For years, whites tried to work out a theory that Great Zimbabwe was built by people other than Africans. This sophisticated series of structures did not fit in with the white settlers' beliefs about Africans as uncivilized, primitive people. But the oral tales that carried the history of a tribe and kept it alive for each new generation successfully conveyed the way things were before their languages gained a written form. In Portuguese writings of the sixteenth and seventeenth centuries, there are references to the structures of Great Zimbabwe.

MUNHUMUTAPA

In the 1600s, the area called Munhumutapa was ruled by Dombo, a Shona and a fierce warrior. He possessed firearms, perhaps from Arab traders who had been to China, and called his elite warrior tribe *Rozvi*, meaning destroyers. Dombo kept his kingdom away from foreign influence but traded ivory and gold to coastal people. He threw out the Portuguese, who had first entered the territory in 1513. The Rozvi were predominantly farmers, but there were also artisans among them who were adept at making objects of ivory, gold, and other metals, all available in the area, as well as pottery.

THE NDEBELE ARRIVE

It was not until 1822, however, that various groups of the
Ndebele began moving northward into Zimbabwe, retreating
from the aggressive Zulus in Natal and the expanding Afrikaner
white farmers to the southeast. The Ndebele were themselves
offshoots of the Zulus and shared with them skill and training in
warfare. They soon came into conflict with the Shona, from whom
they demanded cattle. Dominant among the Ndebele, and
answering to the king, were the *Zansi*, the Zulu warriors who had
left South Africa with their leader Mzilikazi. They traced their
descent directly to the Zulus, known for their fighting ability and
spirit. Beneath the Zansi was a second class of Africans who had
joined the Ndebele on their journey northward. Finally, at the
bottom of the social scale were those Shona who worked for the
Ndebele.

The Shona had an elaborate hierarchy of priests. The Ndebele
had just one high priest, and though the Shona priesthood was set
aside by the Ndebele, they respected Shona oracles as links to local
spirits and fertility gods.

To retain their independence, the Ndebele tried to limit contact
with the Europeans who were eager to increase their territory.
The Shona had followed a similar policy in order to monopolize
external trade. In the 1600s, they had pushed out the Portuguese
traders who had been active in the territory since 1513. European
influence was seen to be corrupting, and inevitably led to the loss
of power by the Africans. But the tide of European expansion into
the area could not be stopped, though the Africans tried to control
it by forcing Europeans to ask permission to enter Ndebele
territory.

Lobengula, king of the Ndebele during the nineteenth century

A NEW NDEBELE LEADER

When Mzilikazi, who led and essentially founded the Ndebele people in Zimbabwe, died, Lobengula was named *ikose*, the king. It was left to Lobengula to bridge the enormous distance between his people and the Europeans who were streaming into the territory looking for minerals and land rights, and offering fraudulent treaties. Inevitably, the Ndebele would lose out to the Europeans. The Ndebele were brave and disciplined, but they lacked the military weapons employed by the Europeans.

THE FIRST WHITES

Until 1890, the territory of Zimbabwe had seen few white visitors. A few Portuguese missionaries had begun their efforts to convert the Africans to Christianity as early as the 1540s, but they

David Livingstone and the boat he used for his explorations on the Zambezi River.

had been forced to depart. The earliest known European to enter the territory of Zimbabwe was a Portuguese, Antonio Fernandes. The Portuguese were successfully trading with the Swahili people on the Indian Ocean coast to the east, but wanted to get to the source of the gold and ivory they craved. Fernandes was sent inland to search for the gold mines. He made several successful expeditions, the first in 1513. He provided us with a written record of Great Zimbabwe, which had been abandoned by its inhabitants the century before.

During the late nineteenth century a handful of pioneer missionary-explorers entered the area, notably Dr. David Livingstone, who was well loved by the people. Dr. Livingstone devoted himself to exploring the region, in particular following the Zambezi River for hundreds of miles, searching for its source. His real mission was to try to put an end to the trade in slavery, a practice that appalled him.

Another missionary, Reverend David Carnegie, arrived in Matabeleland in 1882 and visited the Hope Fountain Mission, which was founded in 1870 by Dr. Robert Moffat, father-in-law of Dr. Livingstone. Like many other missionaries, he soon abandoned his attempts to convert the Africans, but he created a vivid written account of his views on the country. He saw a land that "if properly cultivated, would yield splendid harvests. The soil is very well suited for all kinds of European seeds. You need never be without green vegetables all the year round; and fountains bubble up everywhere."

When we refer to discoveries made by the explorers, we mean the impressions of the first white man to see these wonderful sights. We know that Dr. Livingstone was enthralled when he was taken to see Victoria Falls, because he was able to record, and later publish, his thoughts. As was common with explorers in that day and our own, he named these magnificent African falls to honor his own leader, Queen Victoria. But the people who lived near the great falls in Matabeleland had already named them *mosi oa tunya*, the smoke that thunders. While most of these early missionaries made few conversions and no lasting impact on the lives of the Africans, they and the explorers paved the way for the white settlers who would follow in the 1890s. Before that time, there were no white settlers in the territory, only European and Afrikaner travelers and ivory hunters passing through. The missionaries were the only white people living in the territory.

EUROPE DIVIDES UP AFRICA

It all began to change with the Berlin Conference of 1884-1885. Sitting in Berlin, Germany, thousands of miles away from the territories they were discussing, the Europeans agreed to honor one another's claims on portions of African lands. Often the European governments laid claim to territories that they did not control or even occupy. Boundaries were often vague or left undefined since, in many cases, the geography of the areas was not yet known. In some cases, exploration of the territories had just begun.

The Africans who lived in these colonies had nothing to say about who were to be their white colonizers. They became German "controlled" or British "controlled" by the stroke of a pen. Colonial rule was a concept practiced all over the world. Certain countries, possessing great armies or skillful sailors, and wanting to enlarge their power, would send explorers to find and claim foreign lands. Africa was viewed as Europe's playground, full of people who were considered to be greatly in need of European civilization. Europeans did not expect to find any civilizations already in place. They ignored the African nations that had genuine boundaries, and they did not value the rich cultural life of these people. Because most of the Africans did not have written languages, it was felt they had no genuine history. Because their religion and customs, their dress and appearance were so unlike those of Europe, the Europeans assumed they were inferior, rather than just different. Africa was looked on as a source of raw materials, and eventually as a market for European goods. Some colonizing nations such as France and Portugal saw their colonies in Africa as overseas provinces of the mother country. Great Britain brought the colonies into the Empire. It was said in those days that "the sun never set on the British Empire." That claim was made because Britain had colonies all over the world. But in claiming the territory of the Shona and the Ndebele, Britain was merely staking out land that it was not prepared to

Cecil Rhodes

deal with. That situation was tailor-made for Cecil Rhodes. The British established a claim on the territory when they granted Cecil Rhodes a Royal Charter. It was up to him to invest funds, to bring in people, and to gain wealth from the territory.

CECIL RHODES

Rhodes, an Englishman who had come to South Africa when he was seventeen, was a shrewd businessman who had made a fortune in South Africa's diamond fields. He viewed Matabeleland, home of the Ndebele people, and Mashonaland, home of the Mashona people, as sources of even more mineral wealth, since the territory was rumored to be rich with gold. But he also wanted to fulfill his dream of spreading Britain's influence throughout Africa; from Cape Town, at the southernmost tip of Africa, to Cairo, in Egypt, at the northern end. Rhodes was a dreamer on a large scale, well known for getting what he wanted by any means. He approached the British with his plans and asked them to grant his British South Africa Company (BSAC) a Royal Charter over the territory. It was just the right moment for such a request, since the British did not have the money to develop the territory on their own. Reluctantly, in 1889, they granted the charter Rhodes desired.

BRITAIN'S AFRICAN INTERESTS

By bringing Matabeleland and Mashonaland into the British sphere of interest, Rhodes also would help Britain's leader, Lord Salisbury, prevent the Portuguese from linking up their huge colonies in Africa—Mozambique to the east and Angola to the west. Rhodes's agents already had made treaties with various African leaders, including Lobengula, the Ndebele king, but the two sides had very different ideas about what these treaties promised. For Lobengula—and for African leaders throughout the regions—such treaties were believed to give the British the rights to the minerals in the ground, but not the land itself. In African tradition, these two things were considered totally separate. In fact, Africans did not consider it possible to sell land since it was not owned by individuals, but was, like air and water, for the communal use of all the people. But Rhodes, using two different versions of the treaty, one written in English and one oral, told Lobengula he was signing away certain rights in exchange for goods and services, while in fact Rhodes was taking all the rights, including the power to govern a large part of Mashonaland. By such devious means the Europeans made their entry into what would become Rhodesia and, eventually, Zimbabwe.

Frederick Selous (left) and Colonel Starr Jameson (right)

THE 1890 PIONEER COLUMN

In 1890, Cecil Rhodes sent out the Pioneer Column of white settlers, led by Colonel Starr Jameson, into a territory that had been scouted by Frederick Selous. Selous knew Lobengula and he knew the territory. He had visited the area as a hunter when he was eighteen and had scouted there for some twenty years. His findings set the stage for Jameson's trek.

The Pioneers, numbering fewer than two hundred, had been selected from two thousand candidates and were considered not only the elite, but also represented every trade that Rhodes thought would be needed. He expected to create a permanent settlement in the territory and had promised each person 3,000 acres (809 hectares) of land, to be taken from the people who already lived on it. With five hundred mounted police to guard them, the pioneers trekked by ox wagon some 435 miles (700 kilometers), across the Limpopo River into Mashonaland, skirting

The Pioneer Column of white settlers sent out by Cecil Rhodes

the Matabele homeland, where they established Fort Salisbury at a site known to the Africans as Harare. Rhodes expected the pioneers to begin reaping great wealth for his company.

Once established in the area, the pioneers soon discovered that though there was gold, it was deep below the water level and would require expensive pumping and elevator machinery. Although the Africans had worked these mines for hundreds of years, they had cleaned out all the upper-level gold ore. The pioneers were very disappointed and turned their efforts to other kinds of businesses, notably farming, using large numbers of unpaid or poorly paid African labor. (While this original group ignored the gold mines, others would soon take them over; through the following decades, considerable amounts of gold were mined.) When the Pioneer Column moved northward, the Africans honored the treaties and did not attack. But occasional raiding and tribute demands took place between the Ndebele and the Shona, who were always at odds with one another. In 1893, the Ndebele were provoked into a battle that the BSAC inevitably needed to provide plunder to reward the white settlers. In order to "contain" the blacks, and open new lands to Europeans, Native Reserves were established. The blacks in the area were forced to leave their farms and homes and move into these areas designated by the whites.

In 1896, the Shona rose up in rebellion against company rule. They were reacting against forced labor, new taxes, land seizures, and white racial arrogance. Many whites were killed on their farms and ranches before the superior fire power of British machine guns defeated the Africans. The last of the rebels were dynamited in the caves where they had taken refuge. The brutal struggle left a legacy of bitterness and mistrust on both sides in Rhodesia.

By 1902, Cecil Rhodes was dead, but his name and all it represented would continue until 1980.

WHITE SETTLEMENTS

The white settlers, under the Royal Charter granted to the BSAC, took control over every aspect of the country. Most of the best farmland was now in the hands of the company, and was generally acquired by the European settlers and the mining company itself. The British forced some Africans away from their traditional lands. Those who were permitted to stay had to apply for permission to continue to live where they had lived for generations. In the process, the company interfered with the system of chiefs that had been in place for centuries. The chiefs had been responsible for settling all disputes, which they did according to the traditions of their people. The principle they followed was to seek compromise and minimize conflict. Compensation, rather than punishment, was stressed.

COLONIAL RHODESIA

There could not have been two systems more at odds with one another. On one hand was the African social system based strongly on kinship, which stressed the values of communal relationships and sharing. This was contrasted with the European system, which insisted on individual competition. So began a lack of appreciation of the African culture that persisted throughout the colonial period.

Rhodesia's colonial experience, although sharing many of the worst features of racial segregation of South Africa, was unique, largely because the white population was almost entirely British (although there were Afrikaners in the Pioneer Column). This began through happenstance, but was later instituted into government policy. Through the 1890s, Europeans continued to immigrate, reaching a total of eleven thousand by the turn of the century. By 1911, there were twenty-four thousand.

What made it possible for all these people to make the trip from South Africa to Rhodesia was the railroad, an essential part of Rhodes's plan for developing the interior of Africa. The railroad also carried the newly mined minerals. The line from the Mozambique coast near today's city of Beira was started in 1892. It reached Umtali near the Mozambique border in 1898, and Salisbury (formerly Fort Salisbury) in 1899. The second line began from Mafeking in South Africa in 1894, and advanced to Bulawayo in Matabeleland in 1897. By 1902, Bulawayo and

The first train to reach Salisbury in 1899. The railroad was essential in the development of the interior of Africa.

Salisbury were connected and by 1904, a line went all the way to the Zambian border, passing through the important coalfields.

DISTRIBUTION OF LAND

After Rhodes's agents made their biased deals with Lobengula and other native leaders, the blacks were systematically cheated out of their land. A series of land acts deprived them of their traditional lands. They were moved to land that was smaller, poorer, and harder to farm. In 1894, the Native Reserves Act was created. Many of the reserve areas, such as that of the Ndebele north of Bulawayo, had poor soil and insufficient water. Many blacks were compelled to leave lands that were sacred to them. The reserves were patchworks of land, rather than large, integrated units, which could have been farmed in more traditional patterns. The BSAC controlled all unassigned property, including most of the prime farmland in Mashonaland and Matabeleland. The white settlers also took some 250,000 cattle that had been owned by Lobengula. They broke up Ndebele villages, evicted thousands of the Ndebele, and then charged them rent for living on what had been their own land. Hut taxes were imposed on the Africans before 1900. Since the settlers had taken away much of the Africans' way of supporting themselves, the Africans were forced to work at white farms and institutions in order to pay those very taxes. (The whites did not tax themselves at all until 1918.)

From the time Rhodes's company sent out the Pioneer Column in 1890, until 1923, the country was actually run like a company town, with the BSAC making all the important decisions and having complete control over the lives of the people who lived there, not just those who worked for the company. Having received its Royal Charter, and been given permission to run the territory according to a constitution set by Britain, Rhodesia from the start was a strange colony within the British colonial system. Not surprisingly, the company paid little attention to schooling for the blacks. The first schools were not established until 1907, and these were run and funded by the missionaries who had accompanied the Pioneer Column.

During World War I, 2,500 whites and 3,000 blacks from Rhodesia volunteered to serve in support of Great Britain, fighting the Germans in East Africa and helping to occupy South-West Africa (Namibia today).

After World War I, the blacks were crowded into dry, impoverished, and unhealthy reserves, unsuitable for any kind of life. But each of the white men who had fought in the war was given 2,500 acres (1,012 hectares) of Ndebele land. In 1922, 35,000 whites were living in Rhodesia. The 14,763 eligible male voters (thanks to unfair requirements, only 60 Africans among them) were offered a choice between joining the Union of South Africa or gaining status as a crown colony within the British Commonwealth. The voters chose crown colony status by 8,774 to 5,989, ending the years of BSAC rule.

Not content with nearly 30 million acres (over 12 million hectares) of the best farmland, the whites passed the Land Apportionment Act of 1930. This divided Rhodesia, reserving 50.8 percent for the fewer than fifty thousand whites in the country, and designating 7.7 percent (later increased to 22.4 percent) as native purchase areas. The remainder was unassigned, held for future redistribution. All told, three-quarters of a million Africans were now living in the reserves.

A new category, the Tribal Trust Lands, was created in 1969. The country was divided into three types: public lands (6.4 million acres; almost 3 million hectares) and lands for whites and Africans. The whites and Africans received "equal" amounts: 44.5 million acres (19.9 million hectares) for 6 million Africans and 44.5 million acres for 230,000 whites. The Act saw this as "creating parity between the race groups."

Africans were forbidden to live within municipal boundaries; the 900,000 blacks who lived in urban areas had to stay in designated African townships outside the cities and towns.

SELF-RULE

The decision to ask for self-rule under the Commonwealth instead of joining the Union of South Africa was a vote against the Afrikaners, rather than against the racist policies of South

Africa. The British in Rhodesia were afraid that union with South Africa would open the country to an increased Afrikaans-speaking population. They feared vast numbers of such settlers would bring with them a lower standard of living, as well as the Afrikaners' own political ambitions. When Rhodesia was annexed to the crown on October 1, 1923, it had as its Premier Dr. Charles Coghlan, a South African of Irish descent. Although the Rhodesians feared an influx of Afrikaners, it was said that the new crown colony drew many of its administrators and all of its ideas about the natives from South Africa, among them the native registration act and a pass system that made the African a foreigner in his own country.

The British in Rhodesia had no desire to weaken their attachment to Britain; they actually wanted to strengthen it. But they were looking back at a Britain that no longer existed. While political and social ferments were in swing in the mother country, the Rhodesians worked hard to avoid any kind of social change, divorcing themselves from the realities of the present.

WHITE CONTROL OVER RHODESIA

The threat of the Afrikaners having been dealt with, the Rhodesians now turned their attention to subduing the local people. They considered the Africans to be inferior and lacking in ability. The legislation they enacted was specifically designed to prevent Africans from improving their skills and showing their true capabilities.

Rhodesians who had little intellectual development of their own viewed the Africans as little more than animals, to be used for labor. A few whites who were well endowed with wealth,

Dr. Godfrey Huggins

education, and intellect believed the Africans could indeed be absorbed into the culture. Unfortunately for both Rhodesia and the Africans, there were few such people in the country. Most Rhodesian whites would have agreed with the new prime minister, Dr. Godfrey Huggins (later Lord Malvern), who came into power in 1933. He preferred total segregation, but was forced to concede that the blacks were needed for their labor. He evolved a policy in which the unskilled would provide the base of the pyramid in white and black areas, while there would be room for Africans in middle ranks of farming, commerce, and administration within their own segregated community. This scheme held no place whatsoever for highly trained Africans. If the prime minister had been able to push his ideas to the ultimate conclusion, those few who might obtain professional qualification would actually have had to leave their own country, taking their skills elsewhere.

Most of the whites who came to Rhodesia did so in order to find a better life and a higher status than they could have at home. These were the enlisted men who served in World War I, or the younger sons of the landed gentry who would not inherit their fathers' titles or estates. They worked to duplicate the life of an English country gentleman in the Rhodesian bush. Always, they were fearful of being swamped by "outsiders," immigrants from other European countries. As World War II came to a close in 1945, they saw clearly that soon this vast, open country would beckon many whose homelands in Europe had been devastated. Because they wanted to keep Rhodesia for the British, they passed an act in 1946 limiting foreign immigration to between 5 to 10 percent of the British total. By foreign, they meant whites who were not of British ancestry. They were right about the numbers; in the five years between 1946 and 1951, the white population increased by 65 percent, from 82,000 to 135,000. More immigrants came to Rhodesia in the five years following World War II than had come in the previous thirty.

These World War II immigrants had the same vision as those who had come after World War I, a desire to enjoy comforts and a kind of freedom that would be impossible in the Britain of 1945, a country devastated by war. By 1950, the white newcomers outnumbered all who had been born in the country or who had settled there before World War II. It was in such an atmosphere that Ian Smith, a native-born Rhodesian, rose to prominence.

FEDERATION

Following this massive immigration, the whites now set about to protect themselves from yet another threat: the moves toward

black independence that were being felt throughout Africa. A
Central African Federation was proposed, joining Southern and
Northern Rhodesia with Nyasaland (now Malawi) into a political
unit. With white approval only, federation was proclaimed on
August 1, 1953. The whites had described this arrangement as a
partnership with blacks, but only six of the thirty-six members of
the new Parliament were black. When Salisbury was named the
capital of the federation (as well as capital of Southern Rhodesia),
the blacks called it *Bamba Zonke*, which means "take all."

In each of the three countries that made up the federation,
blacks were organizing, pressing for their rights, and trying to
overcome the political systems that were designed to keep them
poor, landless, and voteless.

In 1960, British Prime Minister Harold Macmillan addressed the
all-white Parliament of the Republic of South Africa. In his
famous "winds of change" speech, he said, "The most striking of
all the impressions I have formed since I left London a month ago
is of the strength of this African national consciousness. In
different places it takes different forms, but it is happening
everywhere. The wind of change is blowing through this
continent, and, whether we like it or not, this growth of national
consciousness is a political fact. We must all accept it as a fact, and
our national policies must take account of it." In 1960, seventeen
new countries were born as independent black states in Africa.

IAN SMITH

Ian Smith, who had pushed for federation, was a Rhodesian
deputy party chairman, who, in 1964, became the first locally
born prime minister of Rhodesia. He was a former Royal Air

Ian Smith, the first native-born prime minister

Force pilot who had been severely wounded in World War II and was regarded as a war hero. He voiced the unspoken thought held by many whites in Rhodesia: no majority rule in our lifetime. Within the federation, only Southern Rhodesia remained totally committed to a white minority government, resisting the sure evidence that the winds of change had already blown across vast portions of the continent.

The federation was dissolved when Nyasaland and Northern Rhodesia dropped out. They both gained independence under African governments in 1964: Nyasaland became Malawi and Northern Rhodesia became Zambia. Southern Rhodesia's leaders, however, refused to accept the British government's plans leading to black majority rule. After polling the whites, Smith announced Southern Rhodesia's Unilateral Declaration of Independence (UDI) on November 11, 1965. Britain claimed Rhodesia was still a crown colony, subject to its rule, but would not back this up with military force, proof to the Africans that there was one rule of law for white rebels, another for black.

Rhodesia was now an outlaw state. The world community responded with trade sanctions meant to isolate Rhodesia and cripple it financially, and to force Smith and his followers to give up minority rule. But Rhodesia would prove to be entirely capable of existing under these sanctions, preferring to cope with the restrictions rather than yield to majority black rule.

Tobacco is harvested (below) and brought to the largest tobacco auction floor in the world (above) in Harare, where buyers (below right) inspect the crop.

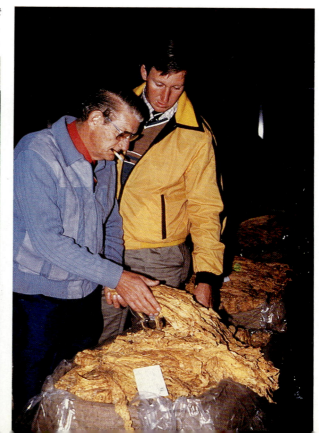

Chapter 4

THE BITTER STRUGGLE
FOR INDEPENDENCE

UNILATERAL DECLARATION OF INDEPENDENCE

Many people truly believed that Rhodesia would not be able to go it alone, as the whites vowed. It was only a matter of weeks, they said, before sanctions "would bring the country to its knees" and Smith would have to accept majority rule along with independence. Actually, Rhodesia was well suited to carry through its plans for self-proclaimed independence, in spite of any sanctions placed on it. Its secret weapon was its bountiful food production.

Sanctions, which prohibited anyone from trading with Rhodesia, were taken up as a challenge by the whites. If no one would sell them textiles, screwdrivers, or the thousands of items needed to run their economy, they would make them at home. As for the prohibition against buying Rhodesian products, the realities of economics overrode moral and political considerations.

Tobacco, Rhodesia's most important crop, was too highly desired to be ignored. The tobacco auctions once had been so open and exciting, they were actually part of a tourist's itinerary. Now they became secret meetings at which tobacco was sold to foreign buyers who feared being seen.

The United States, although nominally a supporter of black rule, found its own way to bypass sanctions to suit its needs. In 1972, an amendment was passed making it legal to import any "strategic" mineral such as Rhodesia's chrome. In force until 1977, this law in effect made the United States a financial supporter of the white government. Oil, the one commodity Rhodesia could not do without, flowed in from South Africa. Portugal, still struggling to hold on to her own colonies in Africa, continued to trade with Rhodesia. When two of these colonies, Mozambique and Angola, gained independence in 1975, South Africa was even more determined to support the breakaway state. If the Rhodesian whites did not retain power, South Africa would be the only white-minority government in Africa.

Through the late 1960s, various plans were proposed to bring Rhodesia back into the world community. But Smith and his government countered with their own proposals, which moved them even farther away from majority rule. One such plan would have guaranteed white domination into the next century.

As the economy struggled forward, Rhodesia came to produce as much as 85 percent of the products it needed to sustain itself. Sanctions were not working. The blacks saw that armed resistance was the only way to force the change from minority to majority rule. Very slowly, in isolated instances, the revolt began, but it was severely limited by a lack of leadership. Although there had been black political organizations working toward majority rule back in the decades before UDI, all of them had been banned by the government. Virtually all the black leaders were imprisoned in 1964, and kept there for ten years.

Joshua Nkomo (left) and President Robert Mugabe (right)

MOVE TO BLACK MAJORITY RULE

Attacks began, targeted first at the white farmers on their widely spaced and vulnerable farms. The first such attack occurred in December 1972; the move to black majority rule can truly be dated from that moment. It took seven years, from the declaration of UDI, for the black resistance movements to organize themselves, to establish bases in sympathetic neighboring countries just outside Rhodesia's borders, and to find countries willing to supply them with weapons. When the West refused to help, the blacks turned to the U.S.S.R., China, and North Korea for military assistance.

In 1974, Joshua Nkomo, an Ndebele leader, and Robert Mugabe, whose followers were mostly Shona, were released from prison, where they had spent the past ten years. Here was the leadership that had been missing.

For the next seven years, the war grew more intense, yet it was the blacks who suffered the most. The number of casualties throughout the period is estimated at twenty-five thousand. Only about three hundred whites were among that number. In death as in life, the ratio of blacks to whites remained constant, about twenty-two to one. Many of the deaths among the blacks were at the hands of the opposing black armies. Nkomo and Mugabe each led armed movements that were divided tribally. Nkomo's Ndebele forces were based in Botswana, near the Ndebele's traditional lands. Mugabe's largely Shona army found shelter in neighboring Mozambique. These two leaders were not only fighting the whites for control of the country, they were also rivals for a position of leadership when majority rule became a reality.

For seven years, from 1972 to 1979, Great Britain as well as the United States tried to work out a transition from minority to majority rule. Always, the plans were thwarted by Ian Smith, who demanded guarantees for the whites that amounted to a continuation of minority rule. While they talked, the resistance forces became better armed, better trained, and bolder. Roads were mined and attacks came closer to the main cities. The white population, never more than 270,000, was losing ground. The nature of the attacks, against a civilian population, made life in Rhodesia a fearful existence for both blacks and whites. Many of the whites were able to escape by leaving the country for the safety of South Africa, Great Britain, the United States, and Australia. The blacks, with nowhere to go and no outside connections, were forced to endure the increasing violence. During those seven years, the white population declined to about 140,000. At least one million blacks were forced to leave their lands and settle elsewhere in Rhodesia.

A tragedy of the war was blacks fighting blacks. Black policemen set their dogs on a crowd (left) in Harare in 1975. In 1977 black security forces (right) stand for inspection.

BLACK ON BLACK

Although the war was a black and white struggle to determine whether the people would remain under white minority rule or win black majority rule, 80 percent of the soldiers in the Rhodesian army were themselves black. Among them was the crack unit, the Rhodesian Rifles. Blacks who had joined the army just to have a job were now fighting against fellow blacks, defending the white-ruled nation.

In addition to the black and white Rhodesians fighting, a small but significant number of foreigners joined in as well. Among them were men from Australia, Canada, and the United States who had fought in Vietnam. They volunteered to fight for the whites in Rhodesia, bringing a unique talent—they knew how to fight a guerrilla war, a war in which the enemy knew the terrain, was fed and hidden by the people living in the country, and who fought on a hit-and-run basis.

THE BUSH WAR

As the two black armies moved around the country, in the *bundu*, or bush, they took everything they needed from the local people: food, shelter, clothing. When the civilians resisted, they were often killed. If it was suspected that they were sympathetic to a rival black group, they also were killed. In an effort to deny supplies to the black armies, the government created protected villages, another concept used in Vietnam. By moving villagers into areas where they could not help the guerrilla soldiers, the government hoped to speed up the defeat of the two black armies. By the end of the war, more than 350,000 black Rhodesians had been moved into these villages. The protected villages were overcrowded, with virtually no sanitary facilities and little or no clean water, all of which bred disease and malnutrition. Although they were located near the villagers' homes so that they could continue to farm their plots of land, the time spent going back and forth, and the curfew that was imposed, simply added to the enormous difficulties of daily life.

In addition, some 850,000 blacks were made homeless because of extensive attacks in isolated areas; their homes, clinics, and schools were destroyed, forcing the people to flee.

In the face of the growing war, the whites kept their faith in Ian Smith. Each year, on November 11, the anniversary of UDI, Smith and his followers held a ball to celebrate "independence."

SMITH STALLS

In the 1970s, Prime Minister Ian Smith participated in a number of meetings with various black leaders. The United States tried to

British Foreign Secretary David Owen (left) and Bishop Abel Muzorewa (right)

find a settlement by sending Secretary of State Henry Kissinger to Africa to meet with Smith. They discussed a plan for an interim government, to be followed by majority rule in two years. Among the blacks who saw this as a stepping stone to true independence was black Bishop Abel Muzorewa, whose more moderate position made him most acceptable to the whites. Other black leaders saw this half step as no step at all. Rather than participate in a sham election, after fighting so long to achieve independence, they refused to participate. A crucial part of the settlement for the blacks barred whites from retaining control of such vital ministries as defense and internal security during the transition to majority black rule. The whites were not prepared to yield on these points, and the talks ended without success. Seeing that they were working against their own best interests, the two bitter rivals, Nkomo and Mugabe, agreed to join forces as the Patriotic Front. While the others talked, they stepped up the fighting.

INTERIM ELECTIONS

Still another try was made in April 1977 by British Foreign Secretary David Owen. This too fell through. While it appeared that Smith would keep talking forever, rather than settle, the war escalated dramatically. The pace of attacks was stepped up, as were the numbers of blacks killed. The whites were leaving in greater numbers. At this point, Smith acknowledged that some settlement was desirable in order to bring the fighting to an end and have sanctions lifted.

In December 1977, talks were begun with three black leaders: Muzorewa, Ndabaningi Sithole, a minister, and Chief Jeremiah Chireau, a traditional tribal chief. Smith hoped that an internal settlement, with one of these three at the head, would guarantee a secure position for whites. If either Nkomo or Mugabe were to gain prominence, he feared whites would lose much of their privileged life. New propositions led to elections in April 1979 to vote on a constitution that still guaranteed whites a virtual veto over any essential changes. Mugabe and Nkomo boycotted these elections.

Election rallies were held all over the country as the blacks looked forward to their first vote ever. They lined up at voting booths wherever they lived and worked, many of them right on the white-owned farms. In a country where 85 percent of the people lived in the rural areas, it was essential to bring the polls to the people.

Muzorewa, as expected, won the election, and he was formally asked to form a new government. Reflecting the undecided nature of this election, the country was now called Zimbabwe-Rhodesia—it had a kind of split personality. Muzorewa actually took over as prime minister, but the United States and ultimately Great Britain refused to recognize this election or to lift sanctions. It was simply a way of "blacking" up the white rule; it did not provide for a genuine transfer of power to the black majority.

Smith's stalling tactic had been successful, but only up to a point. Although he still held the real power, and thus had protected the white minority, the election had not led to a lifting of sanctions.

MAJORITY RULE

Because of guerrilla victories, everyone finally was ready to get down to serious talking. Mugabe and Nkomo agreed to participate in talks that would lead to a genuine election and majority rule. With all the black leaders now participating, the talks had a chance for success. Once a constitution guaranteeing majority rule had been written, the blacks put on the table the issue that had been virtually ignored, yet was crucial to the success of an independent nation: the return of white-owned lands to the blacks. Just as the negotiations appeared to be breaking down over this one vital point, United States President Jimmy Carter promised to provide hundreds of millions of dollars for land purchase. With the British concurring, the agreement was signed on December 6, 1979. Rhodesia had to become legal once more before it could become independent, so it was briefly returned to crown colony status during the transition, under the governorship of Lord Soames (son-in-law of Britain's former Prime Minister Winston Churchill). As soon as colonial rule was reinstated, sanctions were lifted. Finally, the stage was set.

Elections were slated for February 27-29, 1980, with eleven parties represented. Whites had won one concession: they were guaranteed twenty seats in the one-hundred-member Parliament. But this would never translate into anything but a voice in the black-ruled government. United in war, Robert Mugabe and Joshua Nkomo now ran against each other.

Independence celebration (left) after the election (right)

As Mugabe, his wife Sally, and her mother returned to the black township not far from the center of the capital to cast their ballots, the whole nation's eyes were turned to the outcome of the election. In part because of his ethnic group's enormous majority in the country, and because of his genuine abilities, Mugabe won a huge majority of the eighty seats and became prime minister of Zimbabwe. Prince Charles of Great Britain arrived at the Salisbury airport to represent Great Britain at the independence ceremonies. On April 18, 1980, at the stroke of midnight, the British flag came down for the final time. Lord Soames, who had guided the country during this last transition, watched along with Prince Charles and newly elected Prime Minister Mugabe.

The celebrations in the streets expressed the joy of the blacks who not only had made the choice of their own leader, but who now were full citizens of a real country. The Republic of Zimbabwe was now an independent, black-ruled nation, the fifty-first country in Africa.

Left: Prince Charles of England saluting during independence ceremonies
Right: President Mugabe, shown with his wife Sally, received an
honorary doctor of laws degree from Morehouse College in 1983.

ZIMBABWE

When independence was declared at midnight on April 18,
1980, the United States, which had already offered aid for land
development, opened an embassy in Harare. In the first years of
the country's independence, the United States was by far the
largest donor of aid, contributing $350 million.

When Ronald Reagan succeeded Jimmy Carter as president, that
special relationship changed dramatically. The amount of aid was
reduced each year until 1986 when, because of a diplomatic slight,
President Reagan declared that no future aid would be given to
Zimbabwe. The president was supporting South Africa, refusing
to institute sanctions against her. But the Senate, against the
wishes of the president, overrode his veto and placed sanctions on
South Africa.

At the time, Prime Minister Mugabe was addressing the United
Nations in New York. When he learned that sanctions would be

In 1986, in acknowledgment of his personal talents, as well as of his position as prime minister of the newest African nation, Mugabe was named president of the 101-nation Non-Aligned Movement. This organization is devoted to the advancement of countries that profess not to lean toward the policies of either the Eastern Bloc (led by the U.S.S.R.) or the West (led by the U.S.A.). This prestigious appointment helped to focus world attention on Africa in general and Zimbabwe in particular.

Mugabe has been outspoken in his statements about South Africa, believing that it is his nation's duty to help the blacks in that country achieve their independence too. He is prepared to pay the cost of such a position. At the same time, he has encouraged Zimbabwe's own whites to stay in the country, and to play their very important role, particularly in agriculture. His earlier statements about Marxism have not taken a distant back seat to his policies, but he has been very supportive of capitalist ventures. Whites continue to enjoy the privileges of wealth in Zimbabwe. They have retained their farms and play a role in the government as well. Some of this support has been at the expense of the blacks, who are still waiting for the land that was promised them at independence.

Mugabe is determined to learn from the mistakes of other African countries that had great promise at independence, but whose leaders followed inappropriate policies and spent their resources unwisely. "Our society," he says, "is nonracial. The whites are accepted alongside everybody else. We have not reversed the colonial situation because the blacks have power. The whites have kept their wealth, their lands, their positions. They will continue to play their part. If they have skills, it is the skills that count, not the color of the skin, in terms of what the individual can offer the society. If you have a higher level of skill, you deserve more, a higher level of pay. That should be the judgment of individuals, whether they are black or white."

ZIMBABWE AND SOUTH AFRICA

Perhaps the biggest problem facing Zimbabwe outside its own borders is that posed by South Africa. With its great wealth, military power, and determination to remain a minority white-ruled country, South Africa has set itself against the other countries in the region, all of them now majority ruled. In an effort to face up to this threat, the countries that share common borders with South Africa, or whose economies and security are tied to that of South Africa, have formed themselves into a group known as the Front-Line States. They are Zimbabwe, Zambia, Botswana, Mozambique, and Angola.

As a landlocked country, all of Zimbabwe's trade, both exports and imports, must be shipped through other countries. The logical route for such shipments is through Mozambique, to its Indian Ocean ports of Beira and Maputo. But the rail lines in Mozambique that lead to these ports are under constant siege by the rebel forces fighting in that country. South Africa is heavily involved in assisting these forces, in an effort to destabilize the government of Mozambique. This forces Zimbabwe to use trade routes leading to South African ports. This is more expensive, since these ports are farther away, and it forces Zimbabwe to spend money in South Africa.

A bold step toward solving this crucial problem was taken in 1986, when Mozambique agreed to permit a new company called The Beira Corridor Group to protect the route between Mutare

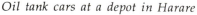

Oil tank cars at a depot in Harare

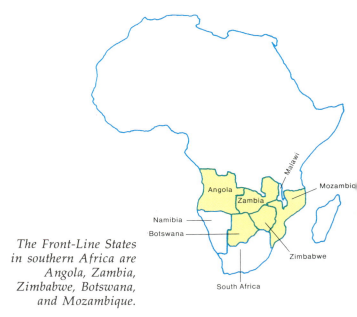

The Front-Line States
in southern Africa are
Angola, Zambia,
Zimbabwe, Botswana,
and Mozambique.

(formerly Umtali) and Beira. The company has created a corridor of land thirty miles (forty-eight kilometers) wide, stretching all the way from the Mozambique-Zimbabwe border to the port city of Beira. Within that corridor lie the railroad, the oil pipeline, a road, and some good farmland. As many as fifteen thousand Zimbabwean soldiers now guard these facilities, making it much safer for goods to be moved.

The Mozambique government, which had lost control of this northern part of its country, hopes the plan will bring peace to the area and allow farmers to return to crucial food production.

The port at Beira, severely neglected because of the ongoing civil war, is being dredged to increase its shipping capacity. Plans have been made to build new tourist facilities in Beira and return it to its place as a tropical vacationland. The increased traffic and the security force should help tourists feel safe traveling this road again, as they did before the war in Mozambique began.

When the pipeline, the railroad, and the port are all operating at full capacity, South Africa will have lost an important economic weapon against its black-ruled neighbors.

The ANC headquarters in Harare after it was raided by South African commandos, war planes, and helicopters in 1986

Zimbabwe has been very forceful in urging that sanctions be applied against South Africa, even though Prime Minister Mugabe knew that his country would suffer as well. South Africa responded with a "go slow" action against Zimbabwe, delaying shipment of goods.

Sanctions are not the only issues facing Zimbabwe in regard to South Africa. Zimbabwe's sovereign territory was violated when the South African army traveled into Harare and destroyed the offices of the African National Congress (ANC), the leading black organization fighting for civil rights in South Africa. The ANC is forced to operate outside South Africa since it was banned there decades ago. The ANC still keeps offices in Harare, and there is little Zimbabwe can do, other than file a diplomatic protest, over South Africa's violation. The country is not prepared to be drawn into a military confrontation with its powerful neighbor to the south. As long as South Africa retains its current political make-up, Zimbabwe will be vulnerable to these aggressive acts.

A nickel mine near Bindura

Chapter 5

THE ECONOMY

INDUSTRY

One of the most pressing needs in Zimbabwe is for jobs—the manufacturing sector cannot expand fast enough to absorb all the graduates coming out of Zimbabwe's schools. In some areas, such as agriculture and mining, employment levels have fallen, but there has been enormous growth in teaching, administration, and service industries. These are the kinds of businesses that require more education, and education is one of President Mugabe's top priorities.

Most industrial production is centered in the two major cities, Harare in Mashonaland and Bulawayo in Matabeleland. Encouraging new industrial development in the other areas of the country is an essential ingredient in providing new jobs in areas where people already live. Zimbabwe has perhaps the most highly diversified manufacturing economy of any country in black Africa, in part because of the restrictions placed on it during the period of UDI.

Workers in a textile plant that produces shirts (left)
and an inspector in a cigarette factory (right)

DIVERSITY OF INDUSTRY

This self-reliant and highly diverse economy calls for a variety
of skills. Iron and steel production, the assembly of automobiles,
household products of every description, paint, paper,
pharmaceutical products, radios and televisions, and a full range
of textile products are among some of the thousands of different
items produced in the country. A textile plant, for example, turns
out shirts for local use, as well as for export to neighboring
African countries. Factories for women's dresses, sweaters, and
shoes, as well as all sorts of household goods that are used in a
modern society were in full production by the time of
independence. Because the fighting did not reach the major
industrial facilities or the cities, the physical plants that produced
all these products remained intact.

ELECTRICAL POWER

Zimbabwe produces much of its own electrical power, relying on the great hydroelectric project at the Kariba Dam on the Zambezi. Zimbabwe and Zambia share in the electricity produced, but since Zambia cannot use all of its share, it sells the surplus to Zimbabwe. Because Zimbabwe is electrifying the rural areas so rapidly (the first time they have had electricity), it needs even more power than can be supplied by Kariba. In 1975, work was started at Hwange on a plant designed to produce steam from the vast supplies of coal readily available in the area. It came on-stream in the mid-1980s, with plans in the works for additional units.

FOREIGN INVESTMENTS

The manufacturing area looks toward foreign investment to increase both the quantity and quality of its products, and to provide some of the new jobs desperately needed. With one major exception, however, foreign companies continue to wait to see if Zimbabwe will be a good place to invest. Their concern has been that President Mugabe would nationalize businesses, in line with his avowed philosophy as a Marxist. In practice, however, Mugabe has worked hard to create confidence in the business community. The manufacturing sector of the economy earns about one-quarter of the gross domestic product. It is the second biggest employer in the country, with 170,600 people, 17 percent of the total work force.

One American company, H.J. Heinz of Pittsburgh, Pennsylvania, has nothing but confidence in the country and applause for its partnership with the government of Zimbabwe. Although its operation there has not resulted in many new jobs (since Heinz bought an existing facility), it has been a great financial success. Sales have increased 124 percent since Heinz took over in 1982.

After a far-ranging search, Heinz found Zimbabwe to be the best economy in sub-Saharan Africa. Heinz's president personally negotiated the company's deal with Mugabe. The profits and products of the plant are not the only benefit to Zimbabwe. Heinz has sent employees to training schools and also has planted experimental crops in order to increase the proportion of local content in the finished products.

Zimbabwe hopes that the example of Heinz will inspire other American companies to invest in the economy as well, since both the host country and the foreign investor benefit from such projects.

MINING

Zimbabwe is well endowed with minerals, which alone give the country a strong economic base. The mines are sophisticated and highly diversified, handling the country's broad range of minerals. It was gold that brought the 1890 Pioneers to Rhodesia and gold is still the most important mineral of the more than forty found here.

GOLD

Gold in Zimbabwe lends itself both to large scale as well as individual operations. Prospecting for gold can be as simple as

An old gold mine (left) and a gold prospector (right)

going out to the bundu with a pick, a pail, and a pan, and working
the soil, washing it with water, and searching for the telltale glints
of gold, just as they do at the Mazoe workings, north of Harare.
The people living in the area centuries ago mined gold
extensively. In 1985, gold contributed 38 percent of the country's
mineral earnings.

The single biggest gold mining company is Lonrho Zimbabwe
Ltd., part of the vast British Lonrho group. Lonrho alone mines
one-third of the nation's gold. (It also is active in forestry,
agriculture, textiles, and engineering.) As mines are worked, the
miners must go deeper and deeper into the earth, calling for large
investments of money to sink the shafts. The price of gold
fluctuates on the open market. In 1986 and mid-1987, it stayed in
the range of $350 to $450 an ounce (28 grams). With total gold
reserves estimated at more than 27 million ounces (765 million
grams), the investment is a sound one.

A copper mine

OTHER MINERALS

Of all the minerals in Zimbabwe, six account for more than 85 percent of the total mineral production: gold, asbestos, nickel, copper, coal, and chromite. Other minerals mined include iron ore, silver, cobalt, and tin, as well as small amounts of limestone, lithium, magnesite, and phosphate. Zimbabwe also mines a beautiful array of gemstones, the most precious of which are the Sandawana emeralds. Mined in the Sandawana Valley, these emeralds are highly prized, according to Maurice Shire, who has made emeralds his life's work. "The mine was discovered about thirty years ago," he says, "and produces the finest emeralds in the world. They are very small but the color is exceptional, a blue green, grass color, and the clarity is extremely good." The mine yields thousands of carats of emeralds a year, most of which are sold to foreign buyers. Other gems include aquamarine, malachite (which is often found near copper deposits), and garnet.

MINERS IN SOUTH AFRICA

Although the mining industry employs about sixty thousand people, men from Rhodesia also went to work in the mines of South Africa, which has been a traditional employer of mine labor from neighboring countries. Although relatively few men went to the mines in the early 1970s, in 1976 there was a huge increase to more than twenty-two thousand men. This peaked in 1977, at twenty-six thousand, perhaps a reflection of the war that was also peaking. Becoming a miner in South Africa was virtually the only way for black men to avoid serving in the war, very often against their will. By the time peace came, the number of miners had dropped as dramatically as it had risen, and by the early 1980s, the number was insignificant.

FARMING

Because their lands were taken away from them through the various land Apportionment Acts and the creation of the Native Reserves, blacks have been promised that they would be resettled on the land and given plots to farm after independence. Slowly, this is beginning to happen.

Black and white farmers in Zimbabwe share the soil but little else, for the tradition of farming, indeed the very purpose of farming, is so different between the two groups. Although the vast majority of blacks do farm, most just do subsistence farming, producing enough for their own families. Some plant enough to have surpluses that they sell at the market. These farms are often worked on communal lands, held jointly by the entire group, or by a clan within the group. In times past, the blacks practiced crop

Many women do the farm labor (left), but a few communities have tractors that are used jointly by a group of farmers (right).

rotation simply by moving on to another piece of land. When they were forced into the reserves, the poorest land in the country, they had no choice but to farm more intensely, overworking the land because there wasn't enough to allow them to move.

The peasant concept of farming is a small-scale operation, using beasts of burden such as oxen when the farmer can afford to own them, otherwise working with just hand tools. This limits the amount of land that can be worked by one family. Some communities now have tractors, which are used jointly by a group of farmers, and this greatly eases the physical burden of the work. However, many men from the rural areas are seeking good-paying jobs in the cities, leaving farm work to their wives.

WOMEN AS FARM LABORERS

In Zimbabwe, much of the work on farms is done by women. Eremina Mvura, a woman from the village of Skiaobvu, works all day to do the chores for her family while her husband is in Harare, studying engineering. In order to provide water, she must

68

first go to the river and carry back the water. Planting, weeding, and all other difficult chores are done by the women, often while they are still nursing a baby. Even those who can afford farm animals, such as oxen to pull plows, must do without because in this area, tsetse flies, which cause sleeping sickness, are still prevalent and kill the animals. The government has embarked on a major spraying campaign to combat tsetse flies, and has cleaned up thousands of square miles of land in the north.

WHITE FARMERS

White farmers work thousands of acres of land in large, commercial operations. Using modern irrigation techniques, taking water from ten thousand private dams, they concentrate both on food crops as well as cash crops. The versatile soybean is used mainly to produce vegetable oil and cattle meal.

CATTLE

Cattle farming generates nearly 20 percent of the country's agricultural earnings, and employs more than seventy thousand people. Cold storage facilities and modern abattoirs enable the country to meet export requirements, guaranteeing that the beef is free from disease. Both domestic and imported cattle are bred for beef.

TOBACCO

Fourteen hundred commercial farms grow tobacco, a crop that alone accounts for 40 percent of the country's agricultural income.

A family in the tobacco fields

Tobacco is a very risky crop because so much can go wrong both during and after the growing. If the rainfall is too little, too late, or even too much, the quality of the tobacco is affected, and its price declines. If the other growers in the world produce a larger crop one year, then the price declines as well. Yet the farmer must still pay the same amounts for seed, labor, and the other expenses that keep his farm going. Tobacco is a crucial cash crop, however, because it earns foreign exchange that Zimbabwe needs to fund its social welfare programs. These tobacco farmers also grow food, including nearly 40 percent of the country's maize. Tobacco and maize crops are often grown in rotation. White farms, whether growing food or tobacco, are enormous by African standards. They use modern equipment and methods, plus a huge amount of black labor. Though there are only an estimated four to five thousand white farmers, they are the largest employer of blacks. While more than half the white population of Zimbabwe emigrated before independence, few of them were farmers.

Mrs. Lovemore with a servant (left) and residents of a colonial family farm (right)

Farmers, of course, cannot take their land with them, a unique reason to stay.

A COLONIAL FARM FAMILY

The ancestors of one such white farm family, the Lovemores, arrived in Matabeleland in 1875 to join the Hope Fountain Mission. Through the generations, they helped build up the country while enjoying the privileged life of the whites. Two of the great-grandchildren became farm wives, one working with tobacco, the other with food crops. They adopted a paternal relationship with the hundreds of black workers and their families on their farms. They distributed food allotments, provided housing, saw that their children were inoculated, and even acted as midwives at the birth of their babies. When Mozambican refugees began flowing into Rhodesia, hundreds took shelter on their farms, moving in with the black workers.

The Lovemores were devoted followers of Ian Smith, attending the annual ball celebrating UDI. But at home, they lived behind

A white family on their tobacco farm (left)
and a white farm owner (right) voting with her workers

barbed wire and taught their children to use shotguns. The husbands and fathers of this family were part of the massive call-up of white men to fight against the blacks in the civil war. One of the Lovemore men, not a farmer, finally gave up on Rhodesia and left for the United States. The rest remain, living as they never dreamed they would, a minority in a black-ruled country. But other than that, very little has changed.

ANGLO-AMERICAN CORPORATION

The single biggest farmer in Zimbabwe is not a person but a company, Anglo-American Corporation, a division of the giant South African firm. This company is said to own about one-fifth of all the land of Zimbabwe, operating enormous tea and coffee estates in the eastern portion, and virtually all of the sugar production in Hippo Valley. Zimbabwe's sugar cane, which provides the raw material for the sugar, is unique in that it is grown far from the sea. Without irrigation, this would not be possible.

Shooting the 1985 remake of King Solomon's Mines

FILMMAKING

Although Zimbabwe has no local film industry, it does have the kind of authentic setting that filmmakers look for: animals in abundance, a beautiful and dependable climate, and thousands of people happy to be signed on as extras for a few dollars a day. A 1985 remake of *King Solomon's Mines* put four thousand extras to work, and brought much-needed foreign exchange to the country.

Although it is historically unlikely, the area of Great Zimbabwe is thought by some to have been the original site of King Solomon's mines, making this an appropriate historical setting for the film. The government is cooperating with movie companies, granting permits and licenses without the kind of red tape that has made working in other parts of Africa too difficult for foreign film companies. Here, when hundreds of authentically dressed

Africans appear over a rise to charge the British enemy, they do so on a landscape that looks like it did in the nineteenth century.

The company that made *King Solomon's Mines* has returned already to make another film. When they move in, they virtually take over a major hotel. When they go home, they have pumped millions of dollars into the local economy and have trained local people in some of the technology of filmmaking. These people are then available to other companies, quickly giving Zimbabwe a reputation as the place to go in Africa to make films.

Other films have been made in Zimbabwe, including *Cry Freedom* about Steve Biko, the South African black activist who died in September 1977. The film was directed by British director Sir Richard Attenborough. Zimbabwe is an ideal site for this film, where there are people whose ancestry is similar to that of Biko. Such a controversial project could never have been made in South Africa itself.

BULAWAYO TRADE FAIR

The annual Zimbabwe International Trade Fair is held each year at Bulawayo, attracting exhibitors from 50 foreign countries. In 1986, nearly 500 Zimbabwean companies showed some of the country's 6,500 locally made items. More than 160,000 visitors attended the exhibition, visiting the 6 major halls at the fairgrounds where the event has been held since 1960.

TOURISM

Zimbabwe offers tourists both familiar and exotic attractions, usually at the same site. The magnificent Victoria Falls, for

Elephants in Hwange National Park

example, is near Hwange, the nation's biggest game park. More than forty thousand elephants still roam the Zimbabwean countryside, so many that the government instructs park rangers to shoot a limited number of them from time to time in order to preserve their own environment. If they did not, the elephants would soon eat their way out of food, causing much wider loss of life. This has already happened in one game park in Kenya, which had a very large elephant population.

Although wildlife is a major attraction in Zimbabwe, residents and visitors both enjoy the water sports at Lake Kariba. Kariba offers the appeal of a great inland sea, the only time the citizens of this landlocked country have been able to look at a body of water that seems to go on forever. Many people used to travel to the Indian Ocean on the shores of Mozambique, but since the civil war began there, that is no longer possible. Instead, they go up to Lake Kariba, just a few hours' drive from Harare, where they can enjoy a weekend "at the shore."

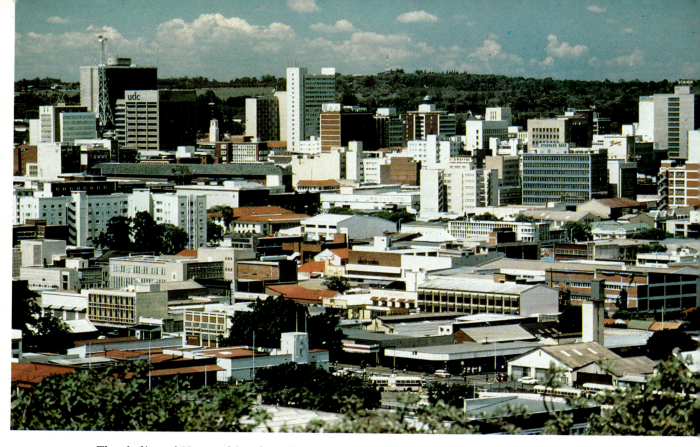

The skyline of Harare (above), a downtown street (below left), and Borrowdale Race Course (below right), a ten minute car ride from the center of town.

Chapter 6

A TOUR OF ZIMBABWE

HARARE

Before independence, the capital city, Salisbury, was a charming little city, lined with jacaranda trees. The streets were filled with small buildings. Only one major new hotel had been built during the fifteen years of UDI, the Monomatapa, named for the ancient Shona king. The central business district was a compact area, easy to cover on foot, although everyone drove their cars right up to the stores where they were shopping.

THE MODERN CAPITAL

Today, the capital city of Harare, named once again for the sloping plain on which it is located, is a bustling city. New construction makes it clear that this is a place where business is conducted. The Borrowdale Race Course, ten minutes away by car, remains as attractive as it was before independence. New hotels

Views of Harare, clockwise from above left: tree-lined Samora
Machel Avenue, street-corner vendors, a traffic policeman,
and a shopping center

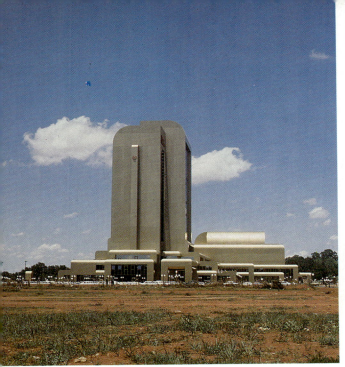

The twenty-one-story Sheraton Hotel (left)
and the Zimbabwe National Art Gallery (right)

include the twenty-one-story Sheraton and the Holiday Inn. The Conference Center, which hosts international meetings, seats 4,500 delegates in its central hall and 650 diners in its ballroom.

Zimbabwe's international airport is just 10 miles (16 kilometers) out of town. Here visitors can catch flights for neighboring countries as well as to London and Frankfurt. The center of town is just 2 miles (3.2 kilometers) from the railroad station.

OLD AND NEW

Older buildings still have their role to play in Harare, in particular the National Archives, which houses the artifacts depicting Zimbabwe's entire history, the National Art Gallery, and the Museum of Human Sciences.

Slums of Harare

Keeping the best of the old is an impressive mark of the new government. Although thirty-two names of towns and buildings were changed in 1982, just two years after independence, they were changed with a great deal of thought. Just as Harare was once the actual name of the site of the city on which Salisbury was built, so too were other names taken from people or places that were meaningful to the area. And, in one case, a name was deliberately not changed because the man it represented, an early administrator, had resigned rather than approve legislation that would cause great hardship for the blacks.

THE SUBURBS AND TOWNSHIPS

The beautiful suburbs, where whites live as luxuriously as they did before independence, are just a short car ride away. In fifteen minutes, beautifully tended gardens, swimming pools, and the look of country living can be seen. The black townships are farther out of town, out of sight of the whites. Although housing is no longer divided racially, economics keep most of the blacks in the same living quarters they have always had. Nearly one million people live in and around Harare.

There may appear to be no differences on the street (above right), but white Zimbabweans usually have much finer housing (above left) than the blacks (below).

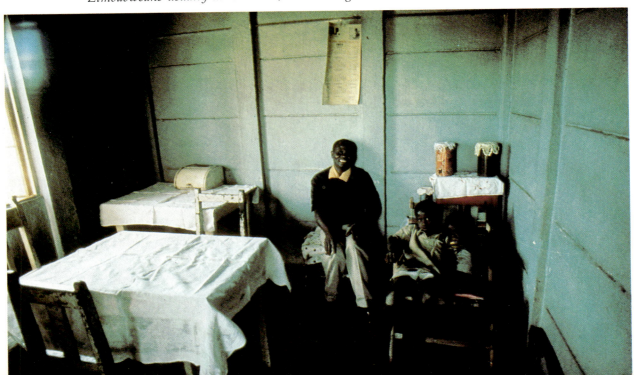

Modern office buildings in Bulawayo

BULAWAYO

Bulawayo is Zimbabwe's second-largest city. Until independence, it was a sleepy kind of town, more African in appearance than Harare. Today it too boasts modern hotels, including the Holiday Inn and the Sun, as well as a technical college and hotel school. Bulawayo is an industrial city, and is host to the annual International Trade Fair that is held in April and May each year.

MUTARE

Mutare is located near the Mozambique border in the beautiful Eastern Highlands. It has the look of Scotland, with green rolling hills and a misty climate. The city is high up in the mountains. Surrounding it are the tea and coffee estates. In the past, Mutare was thought of as Rhodesia's link to the sea, for people would set off from here through Mozambique to reach Beira on the Indian Ocean. The name Mutare is the more authentic spelling and pronunciation of Umtali. That name was really a mistake, reflecting the way whites heard the name "Mutare."

A closeup of housing (above) in a black residential area in Bulawayo (below)

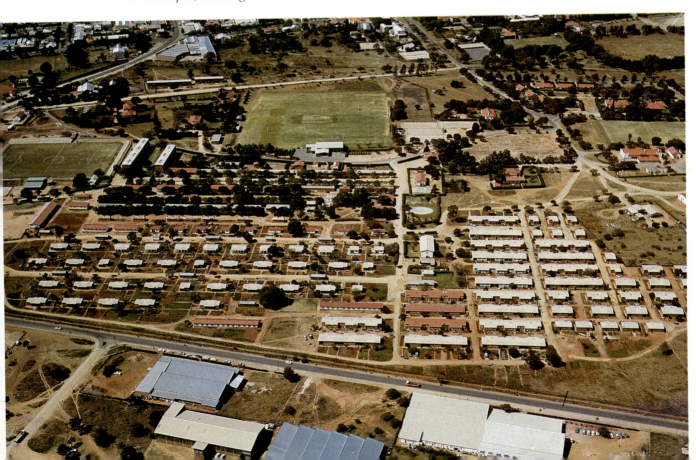

*Kariba Dam (below left) created Lake Kariba (above) in
the Zambezi River and flooded many areas (below right)*

LAKE KARIBA AND THE KARIBA DAM

Fishing people once lived along the Zambezi as it continued on its nearly 500-mile (805-kilometer) journey between Zimbabwe and Zambia. But when the Kariba Dam was built, the lands occupied by the Tonga fishing people were flooded, forming the great Kariba Lake. Much has been written about Operation Noah, in which thousands of animals, whose natural surroundings also were flooded out, were rescued and moved. But little attention has been paid to the twenty thousand Tonga, who had made this riverbank territory their homes for many generations and who shared a close relationship with other Tonga who lived on the Zambian side of the river. When the Tonga were moved, they lost not only their homeland, but their entire way of life. They had never been farmers, but were now moved to lands where they were expected to farm.

The great Kariba Dam was designed and built by Europeans and Africans during the late 1950s to dam the waters of the Zambezi. This created Lake Kariba, a 200-square-mile (518-square-kilometer) inland sea, well known to fishermen for fighting tigerfish, and surrounded by animal and bird life. In addition to providing much needed hydroelectric power, the dam created a great recreational area built around the lake.

Game parks abound in the area, and at Fothergill Island the visitor gets a sense of how the area looked before the dam was built. When the dam was created, the water flowed over the forested land, killing the trees. Thousands of these dead trees remain, standing up starkly in the water, creating an eerie and beautiful sight at sunset. Much of the game viewing is by boat, drifting in and out of the many inlets of the lake. Zimbabwe's

A giraffe (left) maneuvering to take a drink and a rhino (right) nursing her baby

National Parks and Wild Life Estates occupy 11 percent of the country's total land, about 17,425 square miles (45,121 square kilometers).

HWANGE NATIONAL PARK

In the westernmost part of the country is Zimbabwe's largest and greatest game park, Hwange National Park (formerly Wankie). Here, in an area of some 5,650 square miles (14,300 square kilometers), still roam some of the largest elephant herds known in Africa. Although thousands and thousands of them were killed for their great ivory tusks during the last century, visitors can still see a hundred or more at a time at the water holes. Buffalo and rhinoceros are still plentiful. More than one hundred different species of animal are found in the park. During the last years of UDI, visitors who came to the national park were escorted by a machine-gun-toting soldier, for protection—not against the animals but those fighting for their country's independence.

A cruise boat (left) takes tourists to Victoria Falls.
A young visitor to Hwange National Park (right) pets one of the animals.

TOURIST FACILITIES

Zimbabwe offers five-star facilities for tourists. The Monomatapa Hotel in Harare, built before independence, offers the kind of services taken for granted by American travelers: television, radio, and telephone in every room; nightclubs; gourmet restaurants; secretarial services; a hairdresser; and a swimming pool. At the Elephant Hills Country Club in Victoria Falls, visitors find two swimming pools and a casino. They may rent equipment at the hotel and play tennis or golf. The Victoria Falls Hotel is a great favorite with visitors. Sometimes, orphaned animals, such as lions, are found by the park rangers and brought to the hotel grounds. There, in a wooden enclosure, visitors can go in and enjoy a rough-and-tumble session. Although the cubs may be only three months old and like to play like house cats, they're very strong. As soon as they get older and bigger, the rangers take them away; baby claws and teeth can do real damage.

VICTORIA FALLS

A visit to Hwange always includes a drive to the great Victoria
Falls, located just a short distance away. During the height of the
season, when the water flow is at its most intense, 75 million
gallons (284 million liters) leap over the mile-wide falls every
minute, dropping 348 feet (106 meters) into the chasm. The spray
from the water, sometimes reaching more than 1,650 feet (503
meters), is so high that it seems to reach right up to the clouds.
While walking along the paths that rim the edge of the chasm,
visitors wear raincoats provided by the hotels; the mist is as wet
as a rainstorm. A sightseeing airplane ride called the "Flight of
Angels" gives a bird's-eye view of the falls.

When the flow lessens as summer months wear on, the Zambezi

A yawning hippopotamus (left) and the Victoria Falls Bridge (right)

becomes the site for two exciting river trips. For the most adventurous traveler, there are rubber raft journeys down the rapids of the river. These wild and virtually untamed waters can only be navigated for a short period each year, usually starting in September. As they fight to stay upright, the rafters get a sense of the power and fury of the river. But during the quiet times, they can view the game that comes right to the riverbanks.

For those who prefer a quieter kind of river experience, one can paddle a canoe down the Zambezi, traveling as much as sixty miles (ninety-seven kilometers) in three days. This trip starts at the town of Kariba and travels eastward to Chirundu, just before the river reaches the dam. In the river, the traveler will likely see many of the one thousand or so hippos who make the river their home. The canoe passengers have to work hard to paddle around the hippos, who have become very accustomed to these odd human creatures. Other river inhabitants, such as crocodiles, are often seen, giving the paddlers even more of a reason to stay in the boat.

Siskiyou County
School Library

Making pottery at the Mzilikazi
Arts and Craft Center (above),
a wood carver (below left),
and African masks (below right)

Chapter 7

CULTURE

The term "culture" embraces everything that gives people their distinctive history, their style, the way they dance and make music, and the way they decorate their homes and their bodies. Africans are known throughout the world for these characteristics, but not all African people practice all of the arts and crafts.

SCULPTURE

Some concentrate on sculpture, others on music, still others on bodily adornment. Some Shona soapstone carvings, notably birds, were found at the site of Great Zimbabwe; the bird has been adopted as a national symbol and appears on the Zimbabwe flag. With the material at hand, it was natural for these carvings to become the country's best-known art form. Until recently, artists worked on their own. But in the 1960s, a stone sculpture cooperative was begun on the site of a farm near Harare. At one time, as many as sixty-nine people had found their way to the farm and become sculptors—they put their hands and tools to the

African dancers at Victoria Falls

black serpentine rock that was easily obtained on the farm and began to carve. With no training at all, they simply took the material and found in it figures of animals or people. Many of them still work their own farm plots, in order to earn a living, and then come over to the carving co-op at the end of the day to create their sculptures, which are then sold in Harare.

MUSIC

Traditional music has had an especially difficult road to travel. While all central African people make drums of wood and hide and small thumb pianos of scraps of metal, the Zimbabweans also sing and dance to a hand clapping accompaniment.

Drums (left) usually accompany dancers. Students (right) in a marimba band

Like many people around the world, they borrow a great deal from other countries, especially Jamaica. Reggae is virtually the national music of Zimbabwe. Bob Marley, the late singer who brought reggae to the world, was invited to participate in the country's independence ceremonies. High life, the music native to Zaire and Ghana, is popular in the clubs. And Western music fills the airwaves too, often so much so that it is difficult for local musicians to get their work performed.

In 1962, a college of traditional music was opened in Bulawayo. It closed during the war, then reopened. The students are taught classical music in order to learn to read and write notation. This is used as a basis for learning African music. The school also does research into traditional instruments, such as those made of gourds, called calabashes.

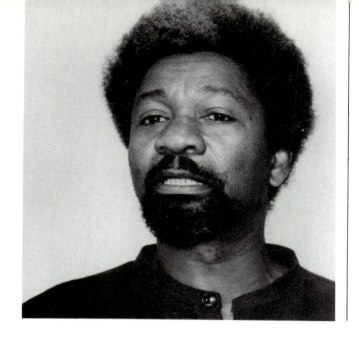

Wole Soyinka, the first African to win a Nobel prize for literature

LITERATURE

Because African languages were not written down until the last century, starting with the arrival of the missionaries, the tradition of storytelling in Africa had been an oral one. An oral tradition can be very rich, but its audience is limited to the people who live nearby. Now that African languages have been given a written form, these storytellers have begun to create a written literature, one that can be read widely by the people who share the languages. Many black writers are published in Zimbabwe, and their books are available in the bookstores there.

In 1986, the first Nobel Prize in Literature awarded to an African went to Wole Soyinka, the Nigerian dramatist, who was given this most important literary prize for the entire body of his work. He said the prize was bestowed on what he represented, "The whole literary tradition in Africa."

For most of us, the literature of Africa has come from European writers, people who lived in Africa and who shared their vision of it in stories, novels, and diaries.

Doris Lessing, who grew up in Zimbabwe, wrote many books depicting life in Africa.

In the colonial period of Rhodesia, one writer gave her adopted country a voice. Doris Lessing depicted the torments of the country in her well-known novel, *The Grass is Singing*. As a keen observer of the injustice being lived every day by the Africans, Lessing notes, "Writers brought up in Africa have many advantages—being at the center of a modern battlefield; part of a society in rapid, dramatic change. But in a long run it can also be a handicap; to wake up every morning with one's eyes on a fresh evidence of inhumanity; to be reminded twenty times a day of injustice, and always the same brand of it, can be limiting. There are other things in living besides injustice, even for the victims of it."

And so she tried to move on from that searing despair, and to present the everyday life she saw about her as well as the pain. "I believe," she said, "that the chief gift from Africa to writers, white and black, is the continent itself. . . . Africa gives you the knowledge that man is a small creature, among other creatures, in a large landscape."

Zimbabwean children

Chapter 8

EVERYDAY LIFE

MARRIAGE AND FAMILY LIFE

While more than a quarter of the blacks consider themselves Christians, many men still practice polygamy, a traditional African practice. Having more than one wife is a sign of wealth in Africa, for the parents of each wife must be compensated for the loss of their daughter with *lobola* (bride wealth). The amount of lobola is set by bargaining between the bride's parents and the groom, and often takes years to pay off. Traditionally, it was paid in cattle; today, it is often paid in cash. The whole tradition of polygamy is changing, both through education and as people become more urbanized. A man with more than one wife must provide a separate house for each, and this requires a certain amount of land.

Of course if some marry more than one woman, others are left with no wife at all. Women are said to prefer this system, for they are entirely dependent on their husbands, and a poor husband would not be able to provide the cattle or seeds for farming. A man with more than one wife may have many children, and children have always been considered a blessing in Africa and a proof of manliness.

African women, who have to bear the children, nurse them, take care of them, pay for their education, and, usually take care of a farm as well, would like to have fewer children. Some of them are beginning to use birth control pills without telling their husbands, who would be very angry. They go to mobile clinics to get the pills and the clinic keeps their records there so the husband will not know. In the past, women would have many children because there was such a small chance that the children would live past their fifth birthdays. But today, with better health care, better food, and clean water, many more children do survive. But for most women, the tradition of having many children has not changed to reflect this higher survival rate, and the population of Zimbabwe has increased rapidly. Each year, the population goes up between 3 and 3.5 percent; at that rate, by the year 2000, there will be twelve million people in the country. More than half the population today is under the age of fifteen. This is the kind of burden no economy in Africa, especially that of a newly independent country, can handle.

SOCIAL SERVICES

With independence, Zimbabwe faced enormous social tasks: illiteracy among adults was high; few children attended school for more than a short time because their parents could not afford to pay school fees. Cattle dips that keep the animals free of disease had been destroyed during the war; roads had been mined during the war and many miles were impassable; rural health clinics had been destroyed. Electricity was virtually unavailable to the blacks, both in the rural areas and the black townships. Clean water had to be provided to help fight the spread of disease.

All of these needs have begun to be met by the new government. In addition, the soldiers who gave up their chance to get an education to fight for their country's independence are now being educated.

TRADITIONAL AFRICAN RELIGION

Although many Africans practice Christianity, and have been educated in mission schools, they may still follow their traditional religions, which have a much longer history. The relationship with one's ancestors is the core of these beliefs; the spirits of those who have died are believed to be very actively involved with the family members who are still living. Disturbing the spirits is believed to bring about natural disasters, such as drought, death of cattle by disease, or diseases that kill small children. Loss of traditional religious sites, such as the Matopos Hills, where Ian Smith chose to place his cattle ranch, are said to anger the spirits. Acting as a go-between for the living people and their dead ancestors are spirit doctors. They can close the gap between the living and the dead, putting them in communication with one another. There are also spirits that govern the land and its fertility. These occupy the bodies of people who are the rainmakers.

A supreme god is recognized by most ethnic groups. The Shona call this being Mwari; the Ndebele use the name Mlimo. Missionaries sometimes use these terms when speaking of the Christian god. Unlike the spirits, this god does not have a life on earth.

Sorcery also plays a role in the life of the Shona, who believe that much of the disease and other ills that visit them are caused

A medicine man in his hut

by sorcerers, who are basically evil, but who may also be moved
to act because of envy of the person they attack. The death of
anyone but an old person is considered to be the result of sorcery.

The Ndebele culture had just one high priest who officiated at
the annual *inxwala*, a great dance, at which the people offered
thanksgiving to the ancestral spirits and showed their loyalty to
their ruler, the king.

MISSIONARIES

In 1829, Dr. Robert Moffat met the Ndebele king, paving the
way for the work of perhaps the most famous of the missionaries,
Dr. David Livingstone. In 1841, Moffat and Livingstone came back
to set up a mission. Livingstone, however, quickly gave up the
idea of a traditional mission. He saw that his medical attention
was much more important to the people than conversion.

Livingstone became one of the foremost explorers in the region, and hoped through this work to open up the country and find a way to end the slave trade.

Livingstone's explorations gave him some insight into the terrible burden slavery placed on the native population. His description of the way it tore these societies apart helped Great Britain reach the decision to make slavery illegal. Livingstone pointed out the paradox of offering Christianity to the Africans while claiming them as slaves.

In their own areas, the Ndebele resisted efforts at conversion. Their own religion was not consistent with Christianity, nor was their way of life suitable for Christian beliefs. With an emphasis on raiding as an essential ingredient of the economy, as well as a society divided into inferior and superior classes, it was not possible to reconcile the two systems of belief.

Christian missionaries only found success among both the Ndebele and the Shona after the establishment of colonial rule. This was a time when traditional African values were being lost in virtually every area of life; losing so much of their culture may have made the people more vulnerable to the missionaries and this new religion.

About one-quarter of the people of Zimbabwe consider themselves Christians. Most people follow traditional religions. However, many Christians also practice the traditional religions of their ancestors. They practice polygamy, for example, which is against the church's teachings but is part of their social fabric.

SPORTS

Zimbabwe is as divided in its sports life as it is in any other area, a reflection of the different ways its black and white people

Lawn bowling

live. The whites' games are typical of the European community: cricket, bowls, golf, tennis, and polo. For these games, private clubs have been set up, with beautifully tended lawns, outdoor bars, and a feeling of being in England. Whites are also keen on target shooting.

For the blacks, soccer is the most popular sport. Skilled boxers compete against other national teams. With independence, Zimbabwe became a participant in the Olympic Games, but it will take years for the country to build up its national teams and to field world-class players such as the runners from Kenya, who are known wherever sports fans gather.

Zimbabwe is one of the few countries in Africa where tourists are permitted to hunt. It is strictly controlled and limited to specified blocks of land, many of them in the north near Lake Kariba. The hunter must apply for a special license and be conducted by a guide.

EDUCATION BEFORE INDEPENDENCE

Like two nations existing separately, yet in the same country, the blacks and whites of colonial Rhodesia were educated in two totally different systems—systems that had different purposes. For the whites, the educational system was designed to produce young people who could lead the country, who would be its doctors, lawyers, and professionals of all types. For the blacks, the educational system was meant to create a suitable group of service people, who could provide back-up services as clerks in the tourist industry, and provide the labor for jobs that whites did not want to do. Certain jobs were reserved for whites, assuring that even educated blacks could not move into these fields.

Almost all blacks were required to pay school fees before independence, but only half of the children from the ages of six to thirteen received any schooling. It was the church missions and local organizations, not the government, that provided much of the education for blacks. Although privately created and funded, these schools still had to meet the standards imposed by the white government.

Many students were educated at farm schools. A typical white farm might employ one to two hundred workers, who brought all their children with them, as many as three or four hundred on just one farm. The farmer's responsibilities to these people included providing whatever housing, sanitary facilities, and schooling they received. For most of these children, what they learned at the farm school was the only education they had.

For whites, however, schooling was not only free, but also compulsory through the age of fifteen, or until graduation from junior high school. Beyond that level, fees were applied for both whites and blacks who wanted to attend high schools. Most whites, with well paying jobs, were able to afford these fees, while most blacks were not. Few blacks entered secondary school and fewer still completed high school.

The only exception to the segregated school system was the

University of Rhodesia (now the University of Zimbabwe). Blacks formed 40 percent of the student body in the 1970s. Although this may seem surprising, it showed that those blacks who were able to get through the levels leading to university had already met and overcome many obstacles, and were clearly eligible for higher education.

EDUCATION TODAY

Changing this system of education posed a truly enormous problem for the new Zimbabwe government. There weren't enough school buildings to bring all the children into the system. There weren't nearly enough trained teachers, books, or other equipment. Even today, school for blacks is not compulsory, since the system has such a long way to go to catch up. Two years after independence, the number of children enrolled in primary schools had doubled, putting more than 90 percent of the six- to thirteen-year-olds in school. There was a lag in the education of the older students, since so few of them had gone through primary education. Two years after independence, fewer than half of them were in secondary school. Many foreigners, especially those from other Commonwealth countries, came to Zimbabwe to teach until the Zimbabweans had enough trained teachers.

All students in Zimbabwe are taught their school subjects in English. Shona and Ndebele were introduced as language courses before independence and now are widespread.

In addition to educating its children, Zimbabwe offers literacy programs to the many adults who had received little or no education in the decades before independence. More than half a million have already learned to read, an important factor in

The University of Zimbabwe in Harare (left) and a rural school

encouraging them to see that their children are educated. Literacy enables both adults and high school graduates to participate in the kinds of cooperatives and small businesses that are seen as the answer to the small number of jobs available to them when they complete their education, in order to avoid the problems of seeing thousands of people migrate to the cities, where there are not enough jobs. The government hopes they will return to the farm areas, and with their new knowledge and ability to read, help the farmers become more productive, creating surpluses that can then be sold to bring in income. Right now, for the ninety thousand students who leave school each year, only seven thousand new jobs are available. The economy cannot expand fast enough to offer employment for all these educated young people.

A village (above) and fishing boats in Lake Kariba (below)

Chapter 9

ZIMBABWE TODAY

AFRICA AGAIN

The immediate gains derived from independence were peace, a chance for the country to take its place as a legal nation, a lifting of all sanctions that had been imposed at the time of UDI, and equality for all races. But Prime Minister Mugabe, his cabinet, and Parliament faced enormous obstacles in obtaining a better life for the black majority while assuring the white minority that their roles in the economy and in agriculture were vital to the success of the new nation.

Although the money promised for land purchase by the United States and Great Britain was received, putting the program into effect proved more difficult than expected. The government had set a goal of settling 162,000 families within four to five years. But before these people could be resettled on the land, there had to be a way to make sure they would be productive. There had to be schools for their children and health clinics nearby; sufficient supplies of clean water had to be provided; and all those needs were expensive. The country itself had to find the money to pay for these projects before the actual land policy could be put into effect. By 1985, 225,000 people had been resettled.

The government enacted a Minimum Wages Act, granting workers in industry and commerce a three-fold increase. Wages of agricultural workers, who were receiving about $17 a month in cash, in addition to housing and food, were increased to $50. Although these wages were still extremely low, farmers in particular complained that they would not be able to make a profit.

Whites continued to leave the country in the first years following independence; the white population declined to fewer than 120,000. Though they had remained throughout the war, some were unable or unwilling to adjust to black rule.

At the same time, Prime Minister Mugabe's plan to provide all the children with an education was faced with a tremendous shortage of teachers, schools, and materials. Many schools had been destroyed during the war for independence. In just a few years, school enrollment rose from fewer than one million pupils in 1979 to 2.5 million in 1985. The number of students attending secondary schools increased even more dramatically.

During the fighting, hundreds of miles of roads had been planted with land mines, making them unsafe for travel and for transporting goods to market. Rural health clinics had been destroyed in the fighting, leaving large numbers of people without any health care. Farm animals suffered killing diseases since the cattle dips that rid animals of insects had also been destroyed.

Two armies, one loyal to Mugabe, the other to Nkomo, had to be disarmed, and then integrated into the regular forces. Many thousands more, not needed in peacetime, were asked to turn in their weapons at specially designated centers, after which they returned to civilian life. Since many of the soldiers were very young, a special education program was devised that would give them a chance to catch up on the schooling they had missed during the war. The success of the demobilization program brought a large measure of security to the citizens.

But no matter how satisfied people were with independence, the Ndebele still found themselves on the outside. It was, perhaps, inevitable that this dissatisfaction would surface. Out in the farthest reaches of Matabeleland, some weapons that had not been turned in were now used to settle old scores. Government troops were sent in to put down the uprising, and after a considerable loss of Ndebele life, they brought it to a halt. It was a reminder that in Africa, as the saying goes, there is only one prize—first prize.

BACK IN THE WORLD

Diplomatic relations with the world community were established: Zimbabwe joined the United Nations, the Organization for African Unity, and the Non-Aligned Movement, of which Mugabe was named president in 1986 for a three-year term. Mugabe also became a leader, along with President Kaunda of Zambia, in the Front-Line States, a group devoted to combating apartheid in South Africa and, in the process, securing their own futures.

Press censorship was lifted to an extent, although the government continues to control both printed and electronic media. Two television channels broadcast a variety of programs, American and British favorites as well as locally produced programs.

UNREST IN MOZAMBIQUE

Hardly had it settled its own war than Zimbabwe had to deal with the problems of Mozambique, with which it shares a very long border. A civil war has raged in Mozambique since shortly after independence in 1975. Because of it, food distribution has suffered greatly. The people in the north of Mozambique, unable to get food, began to stream across the border, entering Zimbabwe as refugees. No one knows how many refugees there are in Zimbabwe, but it is believed that as many as 200,000 people were there in 1986. About one-fourth of that number are in refugee camps run by the United Nations. The rest have settled in with the local population. They slip onto the commercial farms and blend in with the farms' own black populations. On some white-owned farms, as many as two hundred refugees are living with the farm workers and their families. There is no end in sight for the Mozambique war, and many other Zimbabwean farmers continue to take care of the refugees.

PARLIAMENT

In the 1984 elections, Prime Minister Mugabe increased his share of seats in Parliament from fifty-seven to sixty-four. But his major rival, Joshua Nkomo, took all fifteen of the seats in Matabeleland. And Ian Smith, the man who said whites would rule Rhodesia for one thousand years, continued to hold his seat in black-ruled Parliament.

Until 1987, a provision in the Constitution designated that twenty of the one hundred seats be reserved for whites; one-fifth of the Parliament was under the control of .4 percent of the

The last session of the Zimbabwe-Rhodesian Parliament in 1979

population. In 1987, Parliament, including eight of the twenty white members, voted for a constitutional amendment that abolished this provision. Zimbabweans are represented simply as citizens without reference to race.

At the end of 1987, it was announced that Mugabe and his former rival, Joshua Nkomo, had agreed to form a single-party government with Mugabe as president. In January 1988, President Mugabe appointed a new 27-member cabinet and gave key positions to formers foes, including Nkomo.

The status of black women in Zimbabwe remains a difficult problem to solve, one that involves the strength of the people's ties to their ethnic traditions. Mugabe was instrumental in gaining passage of the Legal Age of Majority Act in 1982. It transferred the right to arrange marriages from the parents to the daughter, and allowed women to own property apart from their husbands, as well as to enter into business contracts. But in practice, particularly in the countryside, where 85 percent of the blacks still live, traditional law remains in effect. Parents are unwilling to give up the right to claim lobola for their daughters, and it is still extremely rare for lobola not to be paid.

Zimbabweans, clockwise from above left: classes for teacher training, students at the University of Zimbabwe, spectators at a cricket match, and a young girl

Zimbabwe needs time to educate its blacks for civil service positions to run the many bureaucracies needed by any nation. Its citizens need the luxury of leisure time in order to develop the arts, music, dance, and literature that express cultural identity. It needs time to shake off, finally, the ninety-year colonial history and find its own identity as an African nation in which different ethnic groups have been forced to live together by history.

The countryside in southern Zimbabwe

THE FUTURE

Still, the country remains a bright light in the ranks of independent Africa, one that has come through the first years of post-colonial status in far better shape than had been predicted by many. If the hoped-for foreign investment picks up, many of the programs Mugabe wants to put into effect can be funded, enabling him to fulfill the promises he made at independence.

Zimbabwe is a unique country, formed by its black population as well as by black and white migration. It has been a tribal entity, a chartered company, a crown colony, part of a federation, and an illegal state. Now, as the fifty-first independent African country, it takes its place as one among equals at the United Nations, carrying the name of its great heritage, Zimbabwe.

MAP KEY

Antelope Mine	B4	Marandellas	A5
Beatrice	A5	Masvingo	B5
Beitbridge	B5	Melsetter	A5
Belingwe	B4	Miami	A4
Bikita	B5	Mount Darwin	A5
Bindura	A5	Mrewa	A5
Bulawayo	B4	Mtoko	A5
Chipinga	B5	Mtorashanga	A5
Chiredzi	B5	Mutare	A5
Chirundu	A4	Nkai	A4
Dett	A4	Norton	A5
Enkeldoorn	A5	Nuanetsi	B5
Essexvale	B4	Nyamandhlovu	A4
Figtree	B4	Nyanda	B5
Gokwe	A4	Odzi	A5
Gwai	A4	Plumtree	B4
Gwanda	B4	Rusape	A5
Gweru	A4	Selukwe	A5
Harare	A5	Shamva	A5
Hartley	A5	Shashi River	B4
Highfield	A5	Sipolilo	A5
Hwange	A4	Turk Mine	A4
Inyanga	A5	Umniati River	A4, A5
Inyangani (mountain)	A5	Umvuma	A5
Kariba	A4	Victoria Falls	A4
Karoi	A4	Wankie National Park	A4
Kwekwe	A4	(Hwange National Park)	
Lake Kariba	A4	West Nicholson	B4
Lupani	A4	Zaka	B5
		Zambezi River	A4, A5
		Zvishavane	B5

Cosmopolitan World Atlas, © Copyright 1987 by Rand McNally & Company.
R.L. 87-S-155

4   30°   5   35°   6   40°   7

ZAMBIA

SOUTHERN

Lusaka
Fingoe   TETE
Kafue
Mazabuka   Chirundu
Feira   Zumbo
Chicoa   Zomba
Chioco   MALAWI
Namwala
Monze   Kariba
Gwembe
Pemba
Chipuriro
Mount Darwin
Chinhoyi
Mutorashanga
Shamva   Bindura
Murewa
Mutoko
Harare
Chegutu
Chitungwiza
Gokwe
Kadoma
Beatrice   Marondera
Rusape   Odzi
Kwekwe   Chivhu
Mvuma
Mutare

ZIMBABWE

Nyamandhlovu
Figtree
Turk Mine
Masvingo
Bikita
Bulawayo
Zvishavane
Chipinge
Zaka   Chiredzi
Esigodini
Mberengwa
Gwanda
West Nicholson
Mwenezi

Nata
Serule
Old Tate
Tuli
Beitbridge

Indian Ocean

Blantyre
Chiradzulu
Chiromo
Nsanje
Mungári
Vila de Sena
Vila Fontes
Inyanga
Inhaminga
Vila de Manica
Chimoio
Dondo
Beira
Nova Sofala
Nova Mambone
Bartolomeu Dias
Macovane

Gurue
Alto Molócue
Mocuba
Pebane
Vila da Maganja
Quelimane
Namacurra
Mopeia Velha
Marromeu
Chinde

Nampula
Murrupula
Nametil   Moma
ILHA ANGOCHE
Angoche

ZAMBEZIA

BASSÀS DA INDIA (FR.)
ÎLE EUROPA (FR.)

Morombe
C. ST.-VINCENT

MADAGASCAR

Mabote
Vilanculos
PONTA SÃO SEBASTIÃO
Malvérnia
Mapai
Chigubo
Funhalouro
Massinga
Morrumbene
Maxixe
Inhambane
Panda
Inharrime
Chicomo

GAZA

TRANSVAAL

Gaborone
Pietersburg
Duiwelskloof
Tzaneen
KRUGER NAT'L PARK
Nylstroom
Naboomspruit
Potgietersrus
Ohrigstad
Warmbad
Marble Hall
Lydenburg
Nelspruit
Pretoria
Witbank
Komatipoort
Johannesburg
Germiston
Barberton
Moamba
Springs
Ermelo
Soweto
Carolina
Maputo (Lourenço Marques)
Mbabane
Bela Vista
SWAZILAND
Manzini
Lavumisa
Golela

MAPUTO

Macia
Xai-Xai
Manhiça
Magude
Chibuto
Manjacaze

LESOTHO

Maseru
Durban
Pietermaritzburg

Indian Ocean

45°   40°   7   50°

RMCN.

ÎLES GLORIEUSES (FR.)
COMOROS
Nzwani
Dzaoudzi
MAYOTTE (FR.)

C. D'AMBRE
Antsiranana
C. ST.-SÉBASTIEN
Ambilobe
Vohimarina
NOSY BE
Hell-Ville
Ambanja
Bealanana
Analalava
Antsohihy
Sambava
Doany
Andapa
Antalaha
MAROMOKOTRO 9 436 FT.
ANTSIRANANA
Maroantsetra
C. MASOALA

Mahajanga
Mitsinjo
Soalala
Marovoay
Port-Berge
Ambato Boeny
Besalampy
Mananara
Tsaratanana
Helodrano Antongila
NOSY BORAHA
Ambodifototra

MAHAJANGA

Maevatanana
Andilamena
Kandreho
Morafenobe
Maintirano
Tsiroanomandidy
Ambatondrazaka
Ankazobe
Ivato
Antananarivo
Vohibinany
Antsalova
Ankavandra
Ariyonimamo
Moramanga
Vatomandry
Belo
Miandrivazo
Betafo
Antsirabe
Ambatolampy
Mahanoro
TSIAFAJAVONA 8 671 FT.

ANTANANARIVO

Morondava
Mahabo
Malaimbandy
Ambositra
Nosy Varika
Mandabe
Manja
Ambositra
Morombe
Beroroha
Fianarantsoa
Mananjary
Ambalavao
Manakara
Ankazoabo
Ihosy
Ivohibe
Vohipeno
Farafangana

TOLIARA

Manombo
C. ST.-VINCENT
Sakaraha

MADAGASCAR

Mozambique Channel

Indian

15°   C
25°
30°
20°   D
35°

MINI-FACTS AT A GLANCE

GENERAL INFORMATION

Official Name: Zimbabwe

Capital: Harare

Official Language: English

Government: Zimbabwe is a one-party state. It achieved majority rule and internationally recognized independence in April 1980. The president and his cabinet are responsible to a Parliament, which is comprised of an elected 100-member House of Representatives and an advisory Senate. The Senate includes 40 members; 6 appointed by the president, 24 elected by Parliament, and 10 chiefs. All citizens over 18 are eligible to vote.

There are no regional or state governments. Black mayors were elected for the first time in 1981.

The legal and judicial system is based on Roman-Dutch law.

Religion: Traditional African forms of worship still command the loyalties of a large proportion of the Zimbabwe people. Of the world religions, Christianity is the most popular. The Roman Catholic church has the largest number of adherents. Next in importance is the Anglican church. The major Protestant groups are Methodists and the Congregationalists. Seventh-day Adventists and the Salvation Army have large followings.

Flag: The flag consists of seven horizontal stripes—from the top: green, yellow, red, brown, red, yellow, and green. A white triangle on the left contains a yellow Great Zimbabwe soapstone bird on a red star.

National Anthem: "Ishe Komborera Africa" ("God Bless Africa")

Money: The basic unit of currency is the Zimbabwe dollar. In the fall of 1987, one dollar was worth 38 U.S. cents ($.38).

Weights and Measures: Zimbabwe uses the metric system.

Population: Estimated 1987 population—8,881,000; distribution, 76 percent rural, 24 percent urban; 1982 census—7,550,000

Cities:

Harare (formerly Salisbury)	650,000
Bulawayo	350,000
Gweru (formerly Gwelo)	72,000

Mutare (formerly Umtali) 64,000
Masvingo (formerly Fort Victoria) 35,000
(Population figures based on 1985 estimates)

GEOGRAPHY

Highest Point: Mount Inyangani, 8,514 ft. (2,595 m)

Lowest Point: Sea level

Rivers: The Zambezi River forms the north and northeast boundaries with Zambia, and the Limpopo River forms the border with South Africa on the south. Part of the Zambezi river system includes Lake Kariba, which was formed by the construction of Kariba Dam, and the magnificent Victoria Falls.

Mountains: Zimbabwe is mostly high plateau country, 3,000 to 5,000 ft. (910-1,500 m) above sea level, called the highveld. In Zimbabwe's eastern district along the Mozambique border, a mountain range rises to 6,000 to 8,000 ft. (1,800-2,400 m).

Climate: Although Zimbabwe lies within the tropics, its climate is subtropical. Temperatures vary sharply with altitude. Minimum temperatures range from 37 to 47° F. (3 to 8° C) in winter (September to March) and from 80 to 109° F. (27 to 38° C.) in summer (May to August). Rain falls mainly from about October to April. Floods and severe storms are rare. The climate of the highveld is similar to that of Southern California.

Area: 150,804 sq. mi. (390,580 km²)

NATURE

Trees: Zimbabwe is mainly savanna (tropical grassland) country, with a generous tree growth encouraged by the wet summers. Yet the only true forests are the evergreen forests of the eastern border and the savanna woodland north of Bulawayo, which includes teak. Various species of brachystegia (a hardwood tree with pale reddish-brown wood) are dominant in the midveld and the highveld. Other common varieties include the mohobohobo (a medium-sized tree with large spadelike leaves), the thorn tree, the mopani, and the baobab. Australian eucalyptus have been widely introduced. Jacaranda trees line the streets of Harare.

Animals: Many forms of animal life have disappeared from large areas. Many flesh-eating animals are found in the Hwange (formerly Wankie) National Park; lions, leopards, cheetahs, servals, civets, aardvarks, spotted and brown hyenas, black-backed and side-striped jackals, ratels, and bat-eared foxes. Elephants, gorillas, ant bears, scaly anteaters, giraffes, hippopotamuses, and crocodiles are also prevalent.

Birds: Notable birds are the martial eagle, the bateleur eagle, and the little hammerhead, which builds enormous nests and is revered as a bird of omen.

EVERYDAY LIFE

Food: Maize, the main crop, is pounded into flour to make a dish called *mealies* or *sadza*.

Housing: A severe housing shortage developed in the cities during the seventies due to an influx of rural refugees. The government appealed to private contractors and individual employers to aid in the development of housing for lower-paid workers. Most of the blacks in rural areas live in thatched huts.

Holidays:

> New Year's Day, January 1
> Independence Day, April 18
> Workers' Day, May 1
> Africa Day, May 25
> Heroes' Days, August 11, 12
> Christmas Day, December 25
> Boxing Day, December 26

Culture: The nationalist struggle triggered a renaissance of Shona culture. Herbert Chitepo, who was both an abstract painter and an epic poet, was a forerunner of this renaissance. Stanlake Samkange's novels reconstruct the Shona and Ndebele world of the 1890s, while those of Charles Mugoshi explore the clash of Shona and Western cultures in both the Shona and the English languages. The tradition of oral literature is rich, especially in poetry. Novels center on the conflict between traditional, rural culture and modern life. Doris Lessing depicted the torments of the colonial period in her well-known novel, *The Grass Is Singing.*

Folk traditions have survived in dance and pottery. Sculptors have drawn on tribal religious themes and totems to produce some remarkable works. Particularly outstanding are the sculptures of Takawira and the Tengenenge school of craftsmen who work in hard serpentine. A stone sculpture cooperative has been in operation near Harare since the 1960s.

Musical forms are borrowed from many other countries—especially Jamaica. In 1962, a school of traditional music was opened in Bulawayo.

There is a National Gallery of Zimbabwe, and there are museums in Harare, Mutare, Nyanda, and Bulawayo. The National Archives are one of the major sources for historical material.

Sports and Recreation: For blacks, soccer is the most popular sport. The first sports heroes after independence were the members of the all-white team that was awarded the first gold medal in Olympic history for women's field hockey at the Moscow games in 1980. In general the games enjoyed by the whites are typical of those of the European community: cricket, bowling, golf, tennis, and polo.

Hunting and photographic safaris are available on private game reserves, and the Zambezi River system offers some of the finest sport fishing in Africa.

Communication: The news media are stictly controlled by the government. Radio Zimbabwe broadcasts are in Shona and English. Telephone and telegraph service is available in most of the country.

Transportation: The international airport at Harare has one of the longest civil runways in the world. There are smaller airports in several other cities that can accommodate medium-sized planes.

The main road system is excellent; it generally follows the line of white settlement. Wartime operations brought an improvement in certain areas, including the construction of strategic roads in the eastern highlands and near the Zambian border.

The railroad follows the main road network. It is a single-track line. It is connected to the South African and Mozambican systems to the south and east and to the Zambian system to the north.

Schools: Until 1980, schools were virtually all segregated, and those for whites were generally far superior to those for blacks. Virtually all white children attained both primary and secondary education. Schooling for Africans usually took place in mission schools, and only a small percentage of black children finished. Improvements in education are a high priority of the Zimbabwe government. The University of Zimbabwe had about 1,500 students in 1980, more than half of them Africans.

Health: Before 1980, missionaries had the major responsibility for running clinics and small hospitals. After independence health allocations were increased. Medical and public-health facilities include mother and child care, disease control, environmental sanitation, and rural immunization programs provided through hospitals and district and rural health centers. The burden of disease is greatest on Zimbabwe's youngest children. Malaria is a growing problem, and measles and pneumonia are leading causes of death. Life expectancy at birth: 54 years. Infant death ratio: 74 out of 1,000.

Principal Products:
Agriculture: Coffee, corn, cotton, maize, sugar, tea, tobacco, wheat, cattle
Manufacturing and Processing: Chemicals, clothing, iron and steel, metal products, processed foods, textiles
Mining: Asbestos, chromite, coal, copper, gems, nickel, gold

IMPORTANT DATES

400s—Ancestors of today's Shona occupy the territory

c. 1000-1450—Construction and settlement of Great Zimbabwe

1300s and 1400s—What is now called Zimbabwe flourishes as a ritual and commercial center; gold trade flourishes until the 1700s

1500s—First European contact; Portuguese attempt at conquest begins, but never succeeds

1822—Ndebele move into Zimbabwe

1870—Hope Fountain Mission established by Robert Moffat

1884-85—Berlin Conference settles European claims in Africa

1888—Cecil Rhodes obtains mineral rights from local rulers, including Ndebele king, Lobengula; Rhodes uses these rights as a basis for British South Africa Company (BSAC, 1889) and gets Royal Charter over territory of the Shona and the Ndebele

1890—Rhodes sends Pioneer Column to settle; establishes Ft. Salisbury at Harare

1893—The Ndebele battle with the BSAC

1894—Native Reserves Act forces blacks to live in designated areas

1895—Mashonaland and Metabeleland become Rhodesia under the administration of the British South Africa Company

1896—Ndebele and Shona stage unsuccessful rebellion against BSAC rule

1899—Railroad lines are completed linking South Africa to Rhodesia

1922—Majority of whites vote to gain crown colony status within the British Commonwealth

1923—Rhodesia is removed from BSAC rule; British government permits white settlers internal self-government under the Crown

1930—Land Apportionment Act divides Rhodesia; 50.8 percent of the land for the whites, 7.7 for blacks, and remainder undistributed

1946-51—White population increases from 82,000 to 135,000

1953—Central African Federation is founded consisting of Southern and Northern Rhodesia and Nyasaland (Malawi) to pool resources and markets

1960—Seventeen black African states gain independence

1964—Ian Smith becomes prime minister; black leaders Joshua Nkomo and Robert Mugabe imprisoned

1965—Rhodesia declares Unilateral Declaration of Independence from the United Kingdom; becomes an outlaw state

1969—Tribal Trust Lands are set up, dividing the area into public lands, lands for whites, and lands for Africans

1974—Nkomo and Mugabe join forces as the Patriotic Front; war of liberation intensifies

1979—A new constitution favorable to the minority white Rhodesians is attempted; Abel T. Muzorewa briefly becomes Zimbabwe's first black prime minister, but this is overturned by Britain in the Lusaka Conference

1980—Zimbabwe becomes independent; Robert Mugabe becomes prime minister after free elections

1981—Fighting between rival Shona and Ndebele groups disrupts national unity

1985—Mugabe's party wins elections

1987—Whites lose their reserved seats in Parliament

1988—Robert Mugabe and Joshua Nkomo agree to merge their two political parties, establishing a one-party state, with Mugabe as president.

IMPORTANT PEOPLE

Chief Jeremiah Chireau (1924-   ), a chief

Herbert Chitepo (1923-75), first African lawyer and ZAPU organizer

Antonio Fernandes (in South East Africa from 1506 to 1520s, died c. 1525), Portuguese explorer, first European to enter Zimbabwe

Dr. Godfrey Huggins (1883-1971), called Lord Malvern; prime minister, 1933

Colonel Starr Jameson (1853-1917), used by Cecil Rhodes in military confrontation with King Lobengula

Doris Lessing (1919-   ), author of *The Grass Is Singing*

David Livingstone (1813-73), Scottish missionary and explorer in Africa; discovered Victoria Falls

Lobengula (1833-94), king of the Matabele; defeated in decisive battle with British in 1893

Robert Mugabe (1924-   ), prime minister of Zimbabwe, 1980, president, 1988; nationalist leader

Abel T. Muzorewa (1925-   ), Methodist bishop and first black prime minister

Joshua Nkomo (1917-   ), early nationalist leader and founder of ZAPU (Zimbabwe African People's Union)

Cecil Rhodes (1853-1902), British administrator and financier in South Africa; devoted himself to the development of Rhodesia

Stanlake Samkange (1922-   ), novelist

Ian Smith (1919-   ), first native-born prime minister; took office in 1964

Frederick Selous (1851-1917), a scout who knew the Zimbabwe territory and helped Cecil Rhodes's early settlers

INDEX

Page numbers that appear in boldface type indicate illustrations

hotels, 77, 79, **79**, 82, 87
Hope Fountain Mission, 26, 71, 120
housing, 71, 79, 80, **80**, 81, **81**, **83**, 97, **100**, 103, **106**, 118
Huggins, Dr. Godfrey (Lord Malvern), 38, **38**, 121
hunting, 15, 19, 26, 102, 119
hut taxes, 35
Hwange National Park, 63, 75, **75**, 86-87, 88, 117
ikose, 24
independence, 7, 16, 23, 53, 56, 62, 67, 70, 80, 98, 99, 102-104, 107, 108, 109, 110, 113, 118, 119, 120
independence celebration, 52, **52**, 53, **53**, 93, 118
independence movement, 39-40, 44, 49, 55, 86
Indians, 17
industry, 61-67, 73, 103, 108, 119
interim elections, 49-51
inxwala, 100
Inyanga Mountains, 8, **8**
Inyangani, Mount, 8, 117
iron ore, 66
jacaranda trees, 12, 77, 117
Jamaica, 93, 118
Jameson, Colonel Starr, 30, **30**, 121
Kalahari Desert, 16
Kariba, 89
Kariba, Lake, 10, **10**, 75, **84**, 85, 102, **106**, 117
Kariba Dam, 10, 63, 85, 117
Kaunda, President (Zambia), 109
Khoisan, 19
King Solomon's Mines, 73, **73**
Kissinger, Henry, 49
kopjes, 7
Kutama, 54
lakes, 10, **10**, 75, **84**, 85, 102, **106**, 117
Land Apportionment Act (1930), 36, 120
land distribution, 27, 30, 32, 34-36, 46, 51, 54, 56, 67, 68, 69, 85, 107

land rights, selling of, 29, 120
language, 13, 15, 22, 27, 94, 104, 116
lawn bowling, **102**
Legal Age of Majority Act (1982), 111
Lessing, Doris, 95, **95**, 118, 121
life expectancy, 119
Limpopo River, 8, 19, 30, 117
literacy, 98, 104-105
literature, 94-95, 118
Livingstone, Dr. David, 9, 25, **25**, 26, 100-101, 121
Livingstone, David, Public School, **17**
Lobengula, 24, **24**, 29, 30, 34, 35, 120, 121
lobola (bride wealth), 97, 111
Lonrho Zimbabwe Ltd., 65
Lovemore family, 71-72, **71**
lowveld, 7
Lusaka Conference, 121
Macmillan, Harold, 40
Mafeking, 33
maize (corn), 11, 15, 70, 118, 119
majority rule, 51-52
malachite, 66
malaria, 119
Malawi, 40, 41, 120
manufacturing. *See* industry
maps
    of Africa, **1**
    Front-Line States, **58**
    political, of Zimbabwe, **115**
    relief, of Zimbabwe, **2**
Maputo, 57
Marley, Bob, 93
marriage, 97-98, 111
Mashona, 28
Mashonaland, 19, 28, 29, 31, 35, 61, 120
Masvingo, 20, 117
Matabele, 14-15, 31
Matabeleland, 20, 26, 28, 29, 33, 35, 61, 71, 109, 110
Matopos Hills, 8, 99
measures, 116
medicine man, **100**
midveld, 7, 117
migrations, 19

About the Author

Jason Lauré was born in Chehalis, Washington and lived in California before joining the U.S. Army and serving in France. He attended Columbia University and worked for *The New York Times*.

He traveled to San Francisco and became a photographer during the turbulent 1960s. He recorded those events before setting out on the first of many trips to Africa. He covers the political life of that continent and has also made a number of expeditions across the Sahara.

Mr. Lauré has written about, and photographed in, forty countries in Africa. He has written three books, on South Africa, Portugal, and Bangladesh, in collaboration with Ettagale Blauer. Their Bangladesh book was nominated for a National Book Award.

Mr. Lauré is married to Marisia Lauré, a translator.

Muzorewa, as expected, won the election, and he was formally asked to form a new government. Reflecting the undecided nature of this election, the country was now called Zimbabwe-Rhodesia—it had a kind of split personality. Muzorewa actually took over as prime minister, but the United States and ultimately Great Britain refused to recognize this election or to lift sanctions. It was simply a way of "blacking" up the white rule; it did not provide for a genuine transfer of power to the black majority.

About the Author

Jason Lauré was born in Chehalis, Washington and lived in California before joining the U.S. Army and serving in France. He attended Columbia University and worked for *The New York Times*.

He traveled to San Francisco and became a photographer during the turbulent 1960s. He recorded those events before setting out on the first of many trips to Africa. He covers the political life of that continent and has also made a number of expeditions across the Sahara.

Mr. Lauré has written about, and photographed in, forty countries in Africa. He has written three books, on South Africa, Portugal, and Bangladesh, in collaboration with Ettagale Blauer. Their Bangladesh book was nominated for a National Book Award.

Mr. Lauré is married to Marisia Lauré, a translator.